FALSE ALARM

You're Not Going Crazy, You Have Panic,
AND HERE'S HOW TO SOLVE IT

Jim Lance Woodward, LSCSW

ISBN (print, soft cover): 978-1-7348701-0-7
ISBN (ebook): 978-1-7348701-1-4
ISBN (audiobook): 978-1-7348701-2-1

Published by
Lost Angel Publishing
website: falsealarmbook.com
email: info@falsealarmbook.com

Cover image by
Mark Feiden
The Konza Press www.thekonzapress.com

Praise for *False Alarm*

False Alarm is filled with interesting anecdotes and useful strategies. Woodward has written an extremely readable, practical and informative guide for anyone coping with the distressing effects of panic. He offers a guide for learning how to solve it. I highly recommend *False Alarm* for anyone with panic or those who care about someone suffering from panic.

John Hart, PhD
Anxiety Disorders Consultant, The Menninger Clinic

Whether you are someone suffering from panic attacks or a therapist helping clients who suffer from them, *False Alarm* is a must-read. Jim Woodward's book offers fresh approaches and strategies for addressing the problem of panic. Having seen some of his clients in my own private practice, I can attest that the ideas and techniques presented in *False Alarm* are helping in their lives. This book is most definitely worth reading and I highly recommend it.

Patricia Gleue, APRN
Shunga Creek Mental Health

This is a wonderfully simple, down-to-earth, readable text that provides concrete explanations and recommendations for addressing anxiety and panic disorder. The author has vast mental health experience, and he writes in an open, relaxed style. His vivid case examples are particularly helpful, and he draws and expounds upon the experiences of a rich variety of great thinkers and spiritual traditions that came before him. I highly recommend this book to anyone seeking relief from their anxiety or panic.

Bruce S. Liese, PhD, ABPP
Professor of Family Medicine and Psychiatry, Kansas University

With *False Alarm*, Jim Woodward delivers in his Kansas Midwestern voice a commonsense and right-on-point approach to gaining an understanding of and mastery over anxiety and panic.

Jim comes from an ethos of self-sufficiency, competence, and productivity and with *False Alarm* generously offers a lifeline to promote the same in others. Those whose lives are tragically stymied by catastrophic thoughts and overwhelming feelings that spring from the flood of anxiety and panic so often report with Jim's approach a rapid transformation and life-affirming sense of mastery, confidence, esteem enhancement, and renewal that had come to seem elusive.

Yes, *False Alarm* is a winning strategy, and Jim Woodward is the coach you want in your corner!

Richard Shapiro, PhD
Private Practice

I loved *False Alarm*. It is coherent, concise, and to the point (which I love). I'll use it with all my clients who experience panic. I am quite sure that they will find it very helpful.

Nancy L. Thomas, LSCSW
Private Practice, Dodge City, Kansas

Acknowledgments

Thanks to Mary, my wife, chief supporter, and advisor/writing coach, and to Jennifer and Andrew, our daughter and son, for their encouragement, ideas, and support.

Thanks also to Tom, my IT guy, who keeps me up to date with technology and strategies. I refer to my computer skills as "thinking like the Tom."

Thanks also to my friend Richard Shapiro for his subtle wordsmithing and encouragement.

Thanks also to the Menninger Foundation and all of the invaluable mental health lessons learned so long ago that they are now part of my unconsciousness and to the Beck Institute for their fabulous training in CBT.

Thanks also to Sandra Wendel who is my editor and also a great resource about book publishing, and thanks to Rachel Chrisman, a talented graphic artist and family friend, who designed the book cover and illustrations. And to Megan McCullough for her patient help with the interior layout of the book.

Contents

Introduction

Panic causes untold misery as it did for John, a patient of mine. John started classes at the university filled with excitement and high hopes. But then panic struck. It kept him from attending classes; he rarely left the dorm and dropped out after one semester.

He had many physical symptoms including palpitations, sweating, trembling, shortness of breath, chest pain, and nausea. These symptoms were troubling, but more disturbing was his interpretation of them; he was sure he was weak, going crazy, and that he was no longer himself. He was feeling miserable. He was experiencing panic.

Actually, his problems have no psychotic features, but make no mistake about it, panic can make you feel like you are going crazy. Thankfully he finally reached out for help. Now, he knows what his problems are and is working hard to solve them.

The purpose of this book is to reduce needless suffering.

John's plight is typical of the private agony caused by panic. He will come out of this stronger and better.

As Sigmund Freud said, "Out of your vulnerabilities will come your strength."

Solving panic is actually much easier to do than living with it constantly. This book distills the complex and confusing problem of panic to its essence. The clarity of this approach will give rise to feelings of hope for you, along with a newfound willingness to take on the challenge of solving your panic.

This book—based on my many years of professional experience and success with patients who are like you—will help you understand what panic is and how to overcome yours. We'll explore the following topics:

- What panic is

- How to know if you have panic

- How you developed panic

- Why fighting panic or avoiding it won't work

- Why taking benzodiazepines, like Xanax, will not solve panic

- And the two essential skills you must learn to solve panic

We'll also explore these topics:

- How to keep track of your progress in solving panic

- The purpose and nature of the chemicals driving panic

- What cognitive behavioral therapy is, and why CBT is such a good fit for solving panic

- How to replace the fear of having panic with understanding and facts

- What catastrophic thoughts are, how they drive panic, and how to replace them with rational thoughts (the book provides a menu of realistic ideas that you can choose from to shorten your time in panic)

- How to develop strategies for getting through panic and managing it

- Why panic has been so troubling to you and why it has kept you from living fully

- And why you will experience predictable psychological growth as you solve your panic

1

What Is Panic?

I have never met my patient Fran—face-to-face, that is. She has a professional look on the screen as if she would be comfortable behind a podium or in a boardroom. In reality, she doesn't get out much.

Working from home, she runs a successful internet business tucked away in a small rural town. She participates in therapy via telemedicine, from her computer at home to my laptop at the office. She could not come to my office because of her panic and agoraphobia (her fear of traveling), which actively interfere with her ability to make the commute. Like Fran, many patients with panic develop agoraphobia.

Therapists over the years have helped her in many other ways, but her panic, however, only worsened.

Fran was born to a chemically dependent, drug-seeking mother. Her mother's addiction was severe even when Fran was an infant. It got worse. Her mother was "asleep at the wheel" of parenting, and that is where these types of damaging traumas often happen. The sexual abuse she endured from ages five to ten by her mother's boyfriend was far from the worst of it, Fran told me, adding that her mom must have known. Most people with panic have been through some "stuff"—whether they know and remember it or not.

Her physical symptoms included a racing heart, labored breathing, shakiness, and feeling dizzy. She described her attacks as terrible. Even worse, however, for Fran was that she thought of herself as weak, helpless, and crazy. I thought we—she and I —could solve her panic. Solving panic is a team sport. I knew I had the skills to help her and suspected that she had the motivation to do the necessary work.

Panic is bewildering to people who experience it (until it is understood). Panic is a particular type of anxiety disorder. Anxiety is the most common mental health disorder. Panic is a unique form of anxiety that causes a sudden increase in fear/discomfort related to physiological changes that reach a peak within minutes, and that can come on without reason or warning.

The symptoms are often so distressing that many people go to the emergency room, thinking they are having a heart attack. It is estimated that 25 percent of people who go to the ER for heart problems instead have panic. Some symptoms of panic replicate (or seem like) other medical issues.

During and after a panic attack, people try to make sense of what has just happened to them, and, unfortunately, they often judge the situation to be catastrophically dangerous. Physical symptoms cause scary thoughts, and scary thoughts cause more physical symptoms. In this book, we will untangle this confusing web.

Chemicals released from the adrenal gland cause sudden physiological changes in the body. In panic, the release of these important chemicals simply happens at the wrong time. The ill-timed release of these chemicals is a false alarm. People experiencing panic feel they are in danger. The feelings instantly command their full attention and are commonly interpreted by people as losing control, going crazy, or dying.

People with panic then overfocus on these symptoms, which serves only to escalate them. They become preoccupied with the fear of having another panic attack. Over time, even their involvement with life and relationships can fade, as the fear of panic takes on greater importance. Ultimately, all of this is psychologically expensive and emotionally draining. Panic can cause long-lasting psychological problems. Or it can be solved.

Panic attacks have some of the following physical sensations or symptoms:

- Palpitations
- Sweating
- Trembling
- Shortness of breath
- Chest pain or discomfort
- Choking sensations
- Nausea
- Feeling dizzy or lightheaded
- Experiencing numbness, tingling, chills, or sensations of heat

Isn't it interesting that we can intentionally do many things that cause some of the same sensations? When we do it on purpose, however, these sensations are not at all confusing to us. We can seek out and pay money for many adrenaline-pumping activities such as watching scary movies, going downhill skiing, mountain biking, motorcycle riding, parasailing, riding roller coasters, or skydiving.

We can also do everyday activities such as working out, running to catch a bus, or cheering wildly for a favorite team and experience some of the same adrenaline-producing sensations. During these activities, we barely pay attention at all to what is happening to our bodies. Why is this?

In each situation I just mentioned, the rush of sensations we experience is expected and makes sense; therefore, we do not invite frightening images and feelings in response to them. We don't find these same kinds of sensations to be unpleasant. We think of these sensations as a natural part of the experience.

In panic, however, the stresses we experience and our anxiety about those stressors continue to accumulate. When the total stress load crosses a critical threshold, our survival mechanisms automatically get called into action. The chemicals activate unnecessarily, causing changes and peculiarly timed sensations in the body. These sensations themselves, however, are not the problem.

Thoughts Are the Key

The key to panic is your thoughts about the sensations you're experiencing. Let's see if any of these situations fit for you:

- My panic attacks tend to come unexpectedly, out of the blue some of the time.

- My feelings don't fit with what's going on with the events that are taking place.

- My thoughts and feelings don't make apparent logical sense (and we tend to fear the unknown when it doesn't make sense).

- The situation is scary because the origin, purpose, and nature of these sensations feel confusing.

- I get startled by changes in my body because I don't understand what's happening.

- My sensations are terrifying, and I think I am in danger.

These faulty conclusions are that danger. Fearful thoughts intensify the confusing sensations, thus changing them into symptoms. And when you are experiencing the confusing feelings related to panic, it's easy to misinterpret them like this:

- I feel like I'm going to die.

- I might be having a heart attack.

- I'm losing control.

- This is terrible; I cannot stand it.

- I'm losing my grip on reality.

When a flood of sensations comes out of the blue, we feel frightened. In the search for quick explanations, we tend to jump to the worst-case scenario as a way to explain the confusing sensations. Our bodies then react to these scary thoughts by ramping up the sensations even more. Frightening misunderstandings add more fuel to our survival instincts.

During an actual struggle for survival, this flood of sensations works out well. These chemical changes cause strong reactions in the body too. In an emergency, this would be lifesaving. In actual real-life, dangerous situations, these same reactions can make us stronger, faster, and braver. We can do amazing things, like lifting a car off a child trapped underneath.

It does not work well, however, when these same chemicals release with nothing to fight. Then our bodies pump even more chemicals into the body.

Just like Fran's did, this combination of chemicals and horrific thoughts produces panic. She reacted to the chemicals by thinking of them as proof that she was weak and helpless and probably worthless, too, even though some of the time, she knew better. These days, however, Fran no longer thinks of herself in that toxic way, but instead now identifies herself as a businesswoman. She said, "I like business and solving problems."

A Brief History of Panic

Panic is not a new problem. Both ancient Greek and Latin authors reported cases of pathological anxiety and identified them as medical disorders.

The word *panic* first appeared in 1603. It was derived from the name of the Greek god Panikos who was known to be wild and primitive. He used his power to scare mortals. Panic terrifies people today, as Panikos did then.

Before 1980, anxiety and panic were thought to be neurotic conditions resulting from unconscious and unresolved issues from one's childhood.

Panic was categorized as a separate psychiatric problem in 1980. Panic is a prevalent psychiatric disorder. Two to 3 percent of the population in the United States each year experiences panic. Up to 20 percent have diagnosable anxiety. If you have panic, even though it may feel like you are alone in this, you have plenty of company.

Panic profoundly affects people and changes lives. Real-life examples in this book show the crippling effect panic has on its sufferers. If untreated, panic is devastating; however, it can be treated effectively with excellent therapy. Each of the people in my stories has solved panic—meaning they are no longer afraid of it, have strategies to manage it, and no longer live their lives trying to avoid it.

Two Pioneers in Treating Panic

Aaron Beck, who is the father of cognitive behavioral therapy, outlined the cognitive approach in his book *Depression: Causes and Treatment*, in 1967. He later addressed panic in his book *Anxiety Disorders and Phobias: A Cognitive Perspective*, in 1985.

Before Beck was developing CBT, an Australian physician named Claire Weekes was writing about helping patients solve their panic. Her first book, *Self Help for Your Nerves*, was published in 1962. In another book, *Peace from Nervous Suffering*, published in 1972, Weekes laid out the following approach to treating panic:

- Face the panic.

- Accept the panic (don't fight it).

- Float through the panic, which she described as "masterly inactivity."

- Let time pass.

Her ideas made a lot of sense then and remain relevant today. Weekes was a general practitioner of medicine who had a genuine and profound understanding of panic, as she suffered from the condition. She described fear one as the fear of the precipitating event (like traveling or going to the store) and fear two as "the fear of fear." Fear two is the dread of panic.

Weekes's writings about the treatment of panic fit nicely with today's current cognitive behavioral therapy model for treating panic. She wrote in 1962: "It is important to understand this because your illness is very much an illness of how you think. It is very much an illness of your attitude to fear, panic. You may think it is an illness of how you feel (it almost certainly seems like this), but how you feel depends on how you think, and on what you think. Because it is an illness of what you think, you can recover. Thoughts that are keeping you ill can be changed. In other words, your approach to your illness can be changed."

The writings of Weekes and Beck remain influential in understanding and in solving panic.

2

Do You Have Panic? Find Out. Take the Woodward Panic Test

Stan dropped all his college classes late in the semester, too late for a refund, repeatedly. He was sleeping in and missing class, consciously drinking to die. He was hospitalized but did not change. Smoking marijuana would calm him but interfere with his getting to class.

Stan would set multiple alarms and sleep through them. He was sure his return to class would be awkward and embarrassing, so he avoided both by staying in bed.

To his parents' credit, they hung in with him semester after failed semester. His dad had been harsh with him as a child and was perhaps making up for that by being patient and supportive.

Stan had no physical symptoms of panic—at least none that he had mentioned to me in a therapy session. He thought of himself critically as weak and as a failure.

Sometimes panic is hard to spot. It underlies many forms of suffering. A person like Stan would not be recognized as having a panic disorder based on the physical symptoms of panic alone because he had none. However, he did have thoughts of going crazy during an attack, self-critical thoughts, thinking something terrible was happening; and he did feel terrified, dreaded another attack, and restricted his behavior to avoid being uncomfortable. He also used mind-altering chemical solutions.

We did not know he had panic until I gave him the following panic test. Then our work became much more focused.

The Woodward Panic Test

Assess your panic. Note the number of the following physical sensations listed here that you have that come on suddenly and reach a peak within minutes:

- Palpitations
- Sweating
- Trembling or shaking
- Shortness of breath or smothering sensations
- Chest pain or discomfort
- Choking sensations
- Nausea or abdominal distress
- Feeling dizzy, unsteady, or lightheaded
- Having numbness or tingling sensations
- Having chills or sensations of heat

Also, note the following thoughts accompanying the sensations just listed. Remember: thoughts drive panic.

- Thoughts that things are unreal (derealization) or of being detached from yourself (depersonalization)

- Thoughts that you may be losing control or going crazy

- Thoughts that you might die or have a heart attack or faint

- Having self-critical thoughts related to the symptoms

- Thoughts that these sensations are caused by personal weakness

- Thoughts that something terrible is happening

- Feeling terrified

- Dreading another attack

- Changing or restricting your behavior to avoid another attack

- Using a short-acting mind-altering chemical solution to cope with panic

If you have four of the sensations or thoughts listed, you may have a panic disorder. Two or three of the sensations or thoughts could be a limited-symptom panic attack.

According to the *Diagnostic and Statistical Manual of Mental Disorders* (5th edition), the diagnosis needs to be determined by a mental health professional. To know for sure if you have a panic disorder, see a mental health professional. Medical problems could also cause some of these same issues, so it is advisable to rule out a medical issue by seeing a medical professional too.

This test can be very revealing. I use it to show how these types of thoughts increase panic.

I may ask a question like this: During panic, if you have a thought that you are going crazy or that you are dying, would your body produce more or less adrenaline? If you have panic, the answer is more. Remember: scary thoughts produce more chemicals.

And then I may ask: Do you want to increase panic? Of course, the answer is no. Therefore, you need to begin to think about the sensations of panic in a way that does not make them worse. These discussions hopefully build a basis for starting to understand panic.

I find a racing heart and breathing issues to be the most easily recognizable symptoms of panic. Problems with the heart and breath are threatening.

Stan may have had some physical symptoms of panic when he entered a classroom late, but more troubling to him were his thoughts of feeling ashamed of being so weak and terrified. He believed in rationality, and there seemed to be little of it in how he reacted to these sensations. Stan developed panic in part due to his social anxiety—a fear of a negative evaluation from others.

3

Let's Take an Evolutionary View of Panic (and Thoughts about Our Anxious Ancestors)

I felt a positive connection to Bret when he came to my office as a patient. In part because I had known his grandfather, a popular teacher at the high school both Bret and I had attended although years apart. When Bret was young, due to complicated circumstances, he and his two siblings went to live with his grandfather and grandmother. That was fine until his grandfather died. Then his overwhelmed grandmother became depressed and neglectful. Bret was left to fend for himself and his younger siblings.

By the time I met him, Bret was wealthy and miserable. He thought he was going crazy. His racing heart, sweating, and shaking made him feel a loss of control of his grip on reality. He coped with these attacks by going to the gym. He would stay on the treadmill until he gained control of his breathing. Sometimes he went to the gym three times a day. As a by-product, he was in great shape (and very clean).

He was good at keeping things to himself and getting along by being helpful to others, skills he had learned in childhood. He never complained or called attention to himself. He succeeded in hiding his fear of insanity, but it drained him emotionally.

I helped him understand that he wasn't going crazy; he had panic. I said, "Bret, look out there." I pointed to the woods and creek behind my office building. "Imagine these are ancient times, and we are in a cave looking out there, knowing there are dangerous predators."

"Okay," he played along.

"Now, would it be better to be afraid every day and be anxious and cautious and careful knowing predators could be there even if they weren't or to go out there carefree and risk being killed?"

"Being anxious and worried, I guess," he said.

"So that is the way our ancestors were—anxious. Guess what happened to the ones who weren't anxious?"

"Oh, right," he said.

"They all got eaten!" I affirmed. We both laughed. "All of our ancestors were on the lookout for danger, because they survived, and that is what we inherited."

I said, "We tend to overestimate the risk of things like they did. Their survival depended on not underestimating risk, being on the lookout for danger even when it wasn't there. That is what you are doing with these symptoms of panic. You are overestimating the risk. These are your survival fight-or-flight chemicals that are not dangerous." We discussed this in more detail.

Jessie, also a patient of mine, told me a story about how his fight-or-flight response saved his life. Jessie and a woman were at a secluded area on a local lake. It was late—about the time the area was to close.

A man carrying a gun, a flashlight, and a rope approached them. At first, Jessie thought he was a cop. This was clarified when the intruder calmly said he was going to kill them. Jessie obeyed, and as ordered, he laid on his stomach. He was scared, as men are inclined to be when they feel the cold steel of a pistol pressed against the back of the head. Jessie was still. The man wrapped a rope around one of Jessie's wrists.

Wiping away tears, as he told me the story in my office, Jessie said, "All I could think about was my children. I need to be here for them." Jessie wasn't going to go out that way.

The man with the gun and the light warned Jessie to do as told, or he would be killed.

After a pause, Jessie said, "You can kill me, but you can't tie me up!" as he slowly got up, unsure if he would make it to his feet without being shot and killed.

I thought about what Jessie said, as I heard the story: "You can kill me, but you can't tie me up!" I thought about what Jessie had said, and what he meant. He was implying, I am not helpless! I thought, way to go, Jessie.

During this drama, while the distracted man's attention focused on Jessie, the woman, who had also been lying on her stomach, lunged up and rolled over a short stone fence to escape into the dark. The bad guy yelled in the direction the woman had disappeared, "You just got your boyfriend killed!"

Jessie's fight-or-flight chemicals had now taken over; he began to yell; he walked near the man. Jessie is fierce and imposing when angry, and his fear had turned to anger. Even though the bad guy had a gun, his plan had gone off the rails. The man backed away from Jessie, then ran away.

Our survival chemicals are supposed to work for us—to pump us up to do whatever we need to do. Every day since,

Jessie packs a concealed weapon. He later developed a panic disorder. No doubt, the story just told contributed to a buildup of stressors in Jessie's life that resulted in his panic.

Understanding our survival responses and their role in our evolution can help replace confusion and self-doubt that are common in panic. Those chemicals that helped our ancestors survive are the same ones that get activated during an alarm. Our survival mechanisms are a gift from our ancestors. As my colleagues, Aaron Beck and Gary Emory, have observed, "Nature has provided us with a nervous system that functions exquisitely under ordinary circumstances."

For our ancient ancestors, it proved far better to worry and be afraid of something every day than ever to make the fatal mistake of not being afraid one day and ending up being killed. Beck and Emory wrote, "It is better to have 'false positives' [false alarms] than ever to have 'false negatives' [which miss vital signs of danger] in ambiguous situations. One false negative, and you are eliminated from the gene pool."

We still need our intuitive fight-or-flight reactions, for there are still many dangers and dangerous animals around us today, as Jessie's story illustrates. Some of the most dangerous animals we face are human. We all need our intuitive primitive warning system to keep us safe. These unconscious reactions to danger need to be listened to and honored. However, when these same chemicals are triggered falsely, they may lead to panic.

Imagine a woman waiting alone for an elevator at night in a downtown parking ramp. It arrives and there is just one man in the elevator. She hesitates. Something doesn't feel right. Should she get in the elevator and not risk possibly offending the man? Or pay attention to her warning intuition and the chemicals that go with it? Paying attention to her fear and anxiety can save her life. It gives her subtle but important cues.

No other animal on the planet would get in an iron cage with an animal that poses a risk. Hopefully, neither would the woman.

Our powerful warning signals evolved to protect us—whether we're walking alone in the dark, or exploring a mysterious noise in our home, or peering down a steep ski run. Our alarm system and survival chemicals are there to keep us out of harm's way. They are not dangerous or in any way a sign of weakness. Having anxiety and worry about potential threats is a part of our nature. This tendency to be on alert and looking out for risk is an asset for survival. It helps to keep us safe.

The same powerful chemicals that can be lifesaving when needed are easily misunderstood when they come from stress we have accumulated rather than from a knowable threat. Abstract present-day stresses can trigger ancient survival chemicals. Our bodies are physiologically hot-wired to respond to perceived danger by releasing a cocktail of primitive fight-or-flight chemicals. The chemicals cause sudden changes in the body. Interpreting these sensations as being dangerous is what causes panic.

Conversely, we are on our way to solving panic when we know the nature of those chemically driven reactions and know they can be triggered falsely but present no danger. Knowing the positive evolutionary purpose of these fight-or-flight chemicals and trusting they will not cause harm can begin to help us unravel the mystery of panic.

Our ancestors had healthy anxiety, or they would not have survived. We need a vital balance—enough fear to not get blindsided and enough boldness to take on our challenges.

Jessie's survival instincts came at the right time and saved his life. Bret had the same type of chemicals coming online in his body, but with no danger in sight, he thought he was going mad.

Problem Solving and Accepting Anxiety

Evolution has also favored excellent problem-solving skills. The problem-solving functions of the brain are what we will draw on to solve the problem of panic.

Fear represents a cognitive process—thinking about threats and danger. Anxiety is considered to be an emotional reaction rather than a cognitive one. Anxiety is a heightened state of being on alert.

If we lived in an untroubled world or time with no threats, it would be reasonable to let our guard down and live without anxiety. In actuality, though, we are going to have fears and anxieties. We might as well accept them and try to make them our friend.

Realistic anxiety, based on situations that pose some risk, is a part of a well-lived, adventurous life. Anxiety that does not interfere with performance is not problematic. If a person avoids challenges and opportunities, then certainly some worries could be diminished, as is one's quality of life. The key is to remain engaged with life, with relationships and new experiences, and yet not feel bad about yourself for having anxieties. Having reasonable anxiety is not a sign of weakness or an illness.

Anxiety can even serve to help us perform better, as well as to keep our loved ones and ourselves safe and out of harm's way. It helps us make sure the door is locked at night or that everyone is wearing a seatbelt before driving.

It is better to recognize and "own" our anxieties because denying them costs too much emotionally. Denying anxiety takes a toll on our energy and flexibility; owning and solving anxiety leads to resilience.

Anxiety Can Be Helpful

The best way to explain how anxiety can be helpful is to give you this example: just after graduating from high school, I landed a summer job at a popular swimming area at a local lake.

The swimming area was roped off from the central body of the lake. A long wooden dock spanned the swimming area from the shallow wading end to the deep water. Fifty yards away from the dock, two large barrels floated in even deeper water. Only a cable dotted with small buoys stretching between the barrels separated the swimming area from boats on the lake.

Swimmers frequently tried to swim to the barrels; most but not all could make the journey. Boats of all kinds and sizes would often speed by within inches of the barrels. Water skiers loved to cut at just the right moment and, with a yell, delighted in spraying not only the barrels but also the swimmers.

Kansas has strong southerly winds during the summer. Big winds, big waves, and deep water when combined with tired swimmers presented real, rational risks.

My eighteen-year-old lifeguard self was anxious. Only one of the two lifeguards, however, seemed to be worried: me. The other lifeguard was a twenty-four-year-old guy with many years of experience and a laid-back attitude to go with it.

I experienced two nightmares that made it undeniably clear I was anxious. In one of those vivid dreams, police were pulling a body out of the water. As they maneuvered the bloated gray corpse, my eyes were drawn to the bright plaid swim trunks on it, which seemed oddly out of place with death. I also saw a metallic glint reflected in the bright sunlight. It was a safety pin, with a basket check number, attached to the dead body's swim trunks. To me in my dream, this was a sure sign the dead man had drowned in the swimming area during my watch.

This terrifying thought ended the dream/nightmare with a seeming electric jolt. I was unused to nightmares. I realized how easily and quickly a person could slip out of sight in the waves of the lake and drown. I was only able to get back to sleep by repeating to myself a determined thought, "Not on my watch, not if I can help it!"

During the two summers, we lifeguards pulled eighteen drowning swimmers from the dangerous water. The older lifeguard was technically much better than I. He was much better at the cross-chest carry technique.

Anxiety has a bad reputation in our culture, but sometimes it helps us perform better. Anxiety can sometimes be a good thing. Feeling realistic anxiety can be highly motivating, useful, and lifesaving. I was much more anxious about someone drowning than he was. I was driven by anxiety, worry, and even panic. Because my anxiety made me more alert, I pulled in sixteen of those drowning and panicked swimmers. Thankfully, no one drowned.

Would you rather have a lifeguard watching over your children who was anxious or laid-back?

Fortunately, later, the county commissioners voted to move the swimming area to the end of a quiet cove where there was no traffic from boats or any big waves.

Using Anxiety as a Positive in Therapy

Becky had done poorly during her freshman year in college. Dropping out of college was troubling to her. All of the rest of her family had been academically gifted. She wondered what was wrong. (Her school challenges had been more about difficulties in relationships than any lack of intelligence.)

After serving tacos for a year and a little therapy, Becky was ready for another try at college. I asked her what she wanted to put on our agenda for the day.

She said, "Anxiety about school. I feel it in the pit of my stomach."

I said, "Maybe you need to put a saddle on that anxiety and learn how to ride that pony to help you in school instead of trying to get away from it."

We discussed how, when she feels anxious, it could be a signal that she needs to study and prepare for class. We agreed that, instead of thinking of anxiety as a problem, she needs to escape. She would try to capture the energy of anxiety and use it as motivation to accomplish her goals. She thought it was worth a try and agreed to do so as her homework. We can learn to harness the energy bound in anxiety to accomplish our goals.

She reported successfully using her anxiety as a signal that she needed to study. For the first time she turned in assignments before they were due.

4

Panic Is an Emotional Reaction That Can Be Solved

Jovon was athletic and attractive and had played high school sports. Before panic, she had a job and confidence. After panic, she lost both. Now, she stuck by her mother's side and was irritable most of the time.

In reviewing her symptoms, I asked if she had difficulty breathing. She became annoyed and said sarcastically, "I don't have trouble breathing. It's like I got hit in the stomach with a soccer ball. I can't breathe at all!" Our therapy didn't exactly get off to a great start. Jovon had low expectations that therapy would help her.

Many people with panic become dependent. Jovon was becoming independent until her first panic attack. She agreed to come to therapy at her mother's insistence only if Mom could come too. Dependency and fear of panic had replaced her once active social life.

Cognitive behavioral therapy (or CBT) pays close attention to how people think. It is a rational and verifiable approach to mental health. The main idea is there is an interconnection among thoughts, behaviors, and emotions. It is difficult to change the way you feel, but you can change the way you think.

Thoughts change as you understand things in new ways, and as this happens your feelings will naturally follow suit. This is why cognitive behavioral therapy focuses so heavily on our thoughts. When you change how you think about panic, you will feel less frightened and manage panic more effectively.

If you were a patient in my office, we would look at the following diagram so we could explore how your feelings, behaviors, physiology, and relationships are all an interconnected system impacted by your thoughts.

The diagram is drawn to show how thoughts play a pivotal role in our lives. They also play an important role in both having panic and solving it.

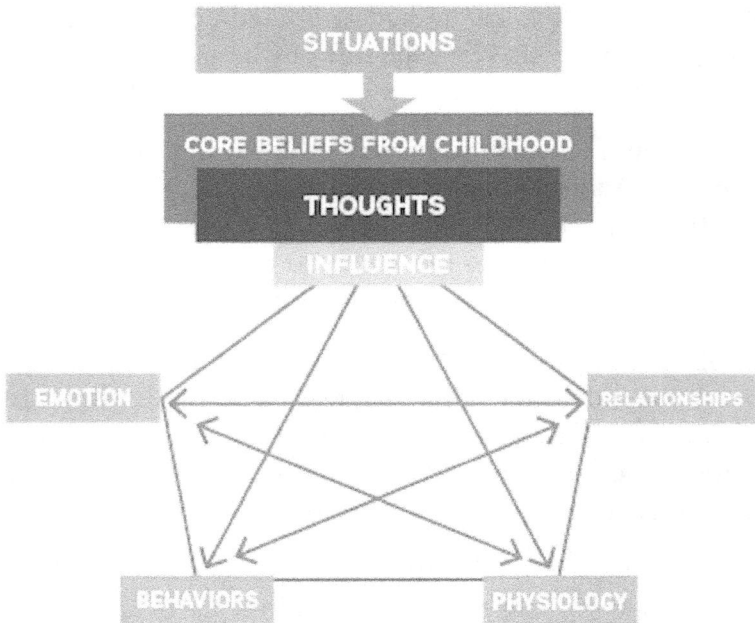

Woodward CBT Diagram

Panic feels like a threat. We react to threats from a primitive survival part of the brain. These functions of the brain are powerful and remain vital to us today; however, they are limited. Our survival reactions essentially only have two gears—to fight or to get away. Problems that don't require an emergency response are not served well by this part of the brain. They are better served by the problem-solving part of the brain.

When the fight-or-flight chemicals release without any apparent reason, and you think, "I must be losing control or going crazy," that process will generate many changes. For example, when panic is triggered, you may experience

- The feeling of fear,

- The behavior of isolation,

- A rapid heartbeat, and

- Dependency on others.

The goal of this work is to change problematic thoughts like "I'm going crazy," to updated thoughts like "This is just a false alarm, and I know how to cope with it." This change of mind will lead to changes in emotions, behaviors, your physiology, and your relationships. For example, you may, instead, experience

- A feeling of confidence,

- Engaged interactions,

- A calm body, and

- Positive connections with others.

Socratic Questions

Changing scary thoughts to more rational thoughts is potent indeed. CBT helps you make these important changes; it also offers a sublime approach to treating panic.

How this process happens is fascinating. A cognitive behavioral therapist will ask many questions about what thoughts you are having. Some questions are just straightforward requests for information known to you. Other questions you may not know the answers to are thought-provoking inquiry (called Socratic questions). These exchanges guide and encourage you to make a shift from reacting emotionally.

A person in panic is reacting from the primitive survival part of the brain. Socratic questions serve to invite thoughtful answers from the problem-solving part of the brain. The purpose of the questions is to help you make a shift from reacting emotionally to responding thoughtfully. This more thoughtful part of the brain, the neocortex, is calmer and less inclined to panic. It is curious and likes to figure things out. So as you answer these questions and think about what is going on, instead of reacting in fear, you are making an important step toward solving your panic.

This is not only thinking in a different way, but also thinking from a different place in your brain. Metaphorically, if we thought of planet Earth as representing the brain, we could think of panic as being a country undergoing an armed revolt. And we could think of solving panic as moving from the area of conflict to solving matters at the negotiating table at the United Nations.

In this section I demonstrate the use of Socratic questions to overcome a variety of cognitive distortions that typically arise with people who are experiencing panic. As you read this, think about which type of cognitive distortions may drive your panic.

Therapists will often ask, "What were you thinking when _____ happened?" It is easy for you not to know the answer to these questions. Frequently we react to situations without necessarily being aware of what thought is driving our reactions. You and your therapist can figure it out. This is just one of the reasons it is easier to solve panic with a wise therapist helping you, although you can do it on your own.

A metaphor I like to use about identifying thoughts is that they are like the scroll at the bottom of a television screen. Imagine you are watching a show and not paying attention to the words at the bottom. The scroll is there whether you are paying attention to it or not.

Our streams of thoughts are like that too. They are there even if they are just out of awareness. You can learn to focus on your thoughts like you can focus on the scroll at the bottom of the screen.

When people don't know what they were thinking before they reacted, I find questions like this to be helpful: "What could you have been thinking that might have led to that feeling or behavior?" (This is a Socratic question.)

Eventually, facts, as understood by your problem-solving brain, the neocortex, can override and calm your emotional reactivity. Active problem solving replaces the terrifying fear that is intrinsic in panic.

Jovon's panic changed the way she thought about herself. Her emotions changed from happy to sad and afraid. She went from working to being unemployed. Physiologically her body became tense and on edge. Worst of all she lost independence and felt fully dependent on her mother. It is common for panic to bring these types of profound changes in people's lives.

Catastrophic Misinterpretations Drive Panic

Naturally, we try to make sense of the significant changes going on in our bodies. Unfortunately, the "sense" we try to make of it frequently makes matters worse. We come up with all kinds of negative ideas. Most people think it feels like some version of terrible. Negative interpretations of symptoms make panic worse and last longer.

The body responds to scary interpretations of sensations by producing more stress-related reactions. During panic, people are "all jacked up" and ready for action, but there is nothing to fight. No tigers. No bears. No bad guys with knives.

Panic invites confusion, until it is understood. Panic attacks and worry about future attacks are so unpleasant and discouraging that they may bring about feelings of hopelessness, insecurity, and depression.

Effective treatment of panic addresses these misinterpretations and creates a real understanding of the actual causes of these sensations. None of the sensations are a threat to life or health. Panic cannot kill you. Having a basic understanding of the biology that causes changes in the body and the brain is essential.

You don't have to be a biologist, but you do have to know and believe that these sensations are not dangerous. The goal of treatment is to stay in a thinking mode during a panic attack. Gaining a fact-based understanding of what is happening in the body during panic is critical to overcoming it.

Cognitive Distortions: Thinking Errors Can Make Panic Worse

Cognitive distortions are distorted views of reality. They are negatively exaggerated thoughts that make panic worse.

Cognitive distortions are like looking at the world through a darkened lens.

During panic, the distorted lens is more like 3-D glasses in a horror movie with images of dying, losing control, and going crazy. The body's reaction to these scary thoughts is to produce more adrenaline. This is not what we want to do. To solve panic it is important to challenge cognitive distortions and to think in more realistic ways, which calms the body.

Here are some cognitive distortions that are common to people who have panic. I've included facts and questions to help you to move away from distorted thinking. They are there to help you move from reacting emotionally to thinking more factually, which calms your body.

Pause and give yourself time to ponder the question and answer it like you would in a conversation. In a real-life situation, answers to any of the questions could turn the discussion in unexpected directions. Therefore, not all of these questions would be asked, and many other questions would take their place.

It seems like these facts and questions would be no match for the power of panic. But panic gains its power when you misunderstand it. These ideas will help you understand panic and gain control over it.

Catastrophizing. Is expecting the worst possible outcome, predicting that something bad will happen. An example of catastrophizing would be that a rapid heartbeat must mean you're having a heart attack.

Facts

- Your doctor said your heart was okay.

- The symptoms of panic are not physically harmful even though they may feel threatening.

- Panic symptoms are caused by survival chemicals that are designed to save your life in an emergency.

- During panic the chemicals are being released at the wrong time.

- If we think scary thoughts, our bodies will produce more fight-or-flight chemicals.

Questions

- Do you believe your doctor that your heart is okay?

- If you think "I'm having a heart attack," would your body produce more adrenaline?

- If you are having a panic attack, do you want more adrenaline? (Usually the answer is an emphatic *no!*)

- If you started thinking about your symptoms as not dangerous, do you think your body would produce less adrenaline?

- How could you think about your racing heart in a different way that would be less frightening?

- Do you understand why that would be so important?

Jumping to conclusions. Expecting that a feared outcome is extremely likely—for example, when anxiety interferes with concentration, you may think, "I'm losing my mind!"

Facts

- Anxiety can interfere with concentration.

- Scary thoughts cause people to produce more of the chemicals that cause panic.

Questions

- Is the thought of losing your mind a scary thought to you?

- On a scale of 1 to 10, how scary is it?

- How much do you believe the thought that you are losing your mind?

- If you knew you were not losing your mind, would that lessen your panic?

- Is the idea of "losing my mind" a fact or a feeling?

- What is more likely? That you are losing your mind or that you are anxious and your anxiety is interfering with your ability to concentrate?

- What is more likely? That you are losing your mind or that you are among the 20 percent of people in the country who have anxiety?

All-or-none thinking. Seeing the world as black or white—for example, "I cannot manage my panic, so I must be weak!"

Facts

- Most people who try to fight with panic feel weak.

- Some people think having panic means they are weak, but really they just don't understand panic.

- When the fight-or-flight chemicals are released into the body, no one can make them go away.

- Fighting panic increases the fight-or-flight chemicals in the body. The only things that make the fight-or-flight chemicals go away are time and relaxation.

- During panic, relaxation does not seem natural, but it helps to shorten the duration of panic.

Question

- Would you like to learn how to deeply relax?

Emotional reasoning. Acting on feelings as if they were facts—for example, someone experiencing a racing heart and difficulty breathing, which feel uncomfortable, may frantically think, "Something terrible must be happening" or "Maybe I'm dying!" Emotional reasoning is thinking if it feels terrible, it must be terrible.

Facts

- The results of the panic test you took show that you have panic.

- Your medical exam said your heart is in good shape.

- A common thought during panic is that you are going to die.

- When the fight-or-flight chemicals are released, they will make your heart beat faster.

- These chemicals are there to help you fight or run away.

- The survival chemicals will not kill you, but they could save your life.

- The chemical surge may feel uncomfortable but is not dangerous.

- A rapid heartbeat during panic is no more dangerous than it is during exercise.

- Our thoughts prompt our physical reactions.

- Scary thoughts produce more adrenaline.

- During a real struggle, the sensations make sense.

- Emotional reasoning is confusing feelings as facts.

Questions

- Is the idea that you might be dying a feeling or a fact?

- Is this the first time you thought you were dying during panic?

- How long did those thoughts last? Did you actually die?

- If you think you might be dying, would your body produce more adrenaline?

- How could you think of these sensations more accurately?

- If you went for a jog, would your heart rate speed up?

- Would you think of that increased heart rate as a sign of danger?

Fortune telling. Thinking as if you can see the future. Like you have a magic crystal ball, programmed to forecast the worst. Two examples of fortune telling are "This is going to be terrible" or "If they know I have panic, they won't accept me."

Facts

- When you have scary thoughts, your body reacts by producing adrenaline.

- Being rejected is a scary thought.

- You think you would not be accepted if people knew you had panic.

Questions

- What are the consequences of thinking you would not be accepted?

- What would be the consequence of believing they would still accept you?

- Imagine I'm your boss and you are telling me about your panic. What you would say?

- How would you feel about a friend if they had panic?

- Have you known anyone else with a panic disorder?

- Did you think less of them because they had panic?

In summary, a main idea in this therapeutic work is to learn to challenge cognitive distortions. Learning to recognize and confront your own thinking errors is an integral part of solving your panic. Do any of the cognitive distortions we have discussed sound familiar?

Symptom	Misinterpretation
Sweating	"Something is wrong with me!"
Trembling or shaking	"I'm losing control of myself!"
Shortness of breath	"I cannot breathe!" "What if I suffocate?"
A feeling of choking	"Something terrible is happening!" "I must be ill!"
Feeling dizzy, unsteady, or lightheaded	"I'm losing control of my body!"
Numbness or tingling sensations	"Something terrible is happening; maybe I'm having a stroke!"
Chills or sensations of heat	"I'm having a medical emergency."

Can you see the common denominator in these thoughts that drive panic?

Five Phases of a Panic Attack

The ideas in this section are highly important. They demonstrate how catastrophic misinterpretations change symptoms from being something minor to full-blown panic.

- First there is an initiating circumstance, which could come from reacting to something in the environment or to something internal.

- Next there is a mildly uncomfortable increase of sensations, like an increased heart rate.

- Then there is an increased focus on these changes in the body. Focusing on the sensations increases them.

- And then, in a search to make sense of the experience, people come up with worst-case scenarios.

- Finally, there is full-blown panic. This happens when the body reacts to these catastrophic interpretations by producing adrenaline just like it would when preparing for a danger.

When there is no real danger present, only an imagined one, people are confused and mistakenly judge the physiological changes to be caused by something terrible. These types of thoughts drive panic. The idea is to understand panic so well that you can skip the last phases of the model. Panic can be averted.

Emotional Reactions vs. Problem Solving

When people are afraid of the symptoms of panic, convincing them that the symptoms of panic are not dangerous is a tough sell for therapists like me. Patients feel terrified and may fear that making any change will worsen symptoms.

One teenager used all of his energy trying to control the symptoms he feared. He revolted against the thought of accepting his symptoms of panic. Instead, he continued fighting to control his symptoms and remained stuck, dreading panic. The idea of facing panic was a bridge too far for him; he dropped out of therapy.

No one wants to be pushed off the diving board before they're ready to make changes. Only with a more accurate understanding will you be willing to experiment with making changes in order to solve your panic. A keystone idea in solving panic is learning that natural, powerful fight/flight reactions are confusing but not dangerous.

Once you gain this understanding, you can begin to loosen the grip of fear and to modify thoughts and images that accompany that fear. Understanding more facts about panic promotes calm. Fear fades. Your willingness to experiment with thinking about panic in new ways will build your confidence. You will find having small successes in managing your panic to be encouraging.

5

Understanding Panic with the Triune Brain Theory

During panic, emotions win out over logic. And in spite of knowing some facts about panic, when the panic chemicals start rolling through their bodies, people react emotionally and let go of their logic.

Let me show you with this conversation:

I asked my patient Maria, "Maria, what was your worst symptom during your last panic attack?"

"The same as it always is. I feel dizzy," she said.

"So how do you interpret your dizziness?" I asked.

"I think there is something wrong with my brain. In spite of all of the times I've been to doctors, all of the tests they have given me, that is still what I think," she said. "I think they just haven't found out what is wrong yet. I think I'm going to die."

"Yes, it sounds like you are stuck in that way of thinking all right. When you think that you are going to die, what happens next to your body?"

She said, "I feel more upset and dizzier."

"Do you want to get unstuck from that way of thinking and feeling?"

"More than anything."

"When you are thinking and feeling like that," I asked, "which part of your brain is in charge?"

"The primitive part," she said.

"I wonder what you would think and feel if that problem-solving part of your brain was in charge—you know, in executive functioning mode?"

She said, "I would feel better. I'd be calmer."

"What would be a more fact-based way to think about your dizziness?"

"Knowing that I'm not in danger. I'd know the blood is flowing from my head and limbs to the trunk of my body so if I was cut, my bleeding would slow," she said. "My body would be trying to prevent me from bleeding to death."

Let's stop the dialogue for a moment and describe what is going on here. Maria does not fully trust her logical understanding. Solving panic is a battle between emotions and logic. As people buy in to logic, panic starts to fade. But emotional reactions don't give up easily. In her battle to solve panic, Maria's emotional reactions are still winning.

I wanted to gauge where she was in this process, so I asked her this question, "What percent do you believe those facts right now?"

She said, "About 70 percent."

I bet it would still be difficult to believe that 70 percent if I asked her that same question when she was dizzy.

I said, "That's good, we are moving in the right direction. Let's keep working on it."

The Triune Brain Model

One way of understanding panic is to know more about the workings of the brain. Paul MacLean, a well-respected neuroscientist, wrote about the structure and function of the brain. He labeled it the Triune brain. His model is a metaphor for understanding how the brain functions. I find that this model fits very well with cognitive behavioral therapy. It is another arrow in the quiver of treatment.

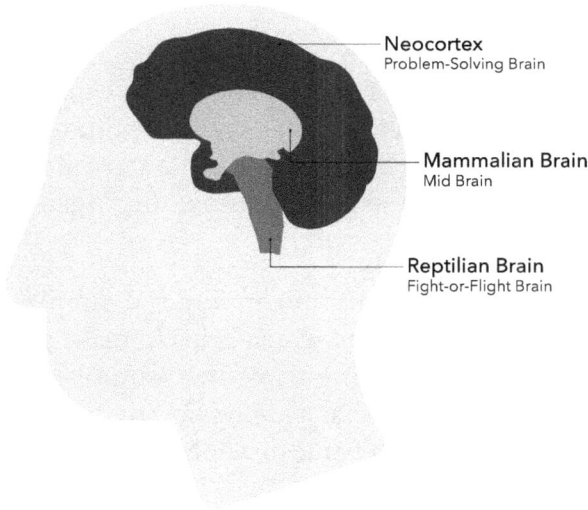

Daniel Segal, a neurologist, has written about the brain and uses what he calls the hand model of the brain to explain the parts/ functions of the brain visually. The hand model of the brain, as demonstrated by Segal, and the Triune brain, as described by MacLean, both represent the same brain structure and functions. According to both models, the brain has three main parts, which evolved through time. The three parts are these:

- The **primitive** or reptilian brain, which we could think of as the fight/flight or survival brain, allows us to be territorial and aggressive. We are functioning from our primitive brain when we believe we are threatened, as in panic.

- The **midbrain** or mammal brain functions include nurturing and connecting emotionally with others, just as mammals do with their young.

- The **neocortex** or problem-solving part of the brain occupies five-sixth of the volume of the brain. When we are functioning from the neocortex, we can problem solve, we can plan effectively, and we enjoy advanced cognition.

Segal presents a model of the brain by using a hand. The heel of the palm represents the primitive brain; the thumb lies across the palm and represents the mammalian or midbrain. The fingers fold over the top of the thumb; the fingers represent the neocortex.

The hand model of the brain provides a simple physical representation of the brain, which helps to make sense of the confusion of panic. During panic the primitive part of the brain takes over. It does what it knows how to do—it fuels us to fight or get away. During panic this only makes matters worse.

Panic attacks take place in the primitive brain. When we perceive a threat, we automatically go to the fight/flight part of our brain. Panic is cured, not by fighting or fleeing, but by problem solving. One goal of treating panic is to bring this more thoughtful and calm problem-solving part of the brain online.

This treatment promotes many factual ways to understand that the symptoms of panic are not dangerous, and it encourages developing strategies to navigate panic. Both of these tasks require problem solving. Making this shift to the rational part of the brain is essential in solving panic.

Understanding the physiology of what is happening during panic and having a strategy to manage it works far better than reacting in fear.

As Maria buys into and believes the idea that she has panic and it is not dangerous, she is making a shift from fight-or-flight reactions to the problem-solving part of her brain. Maria is in the process of updating how she thinks about panic instead of just reacting in fear.

As you learn more about panic and know your symptoms are not a sign of impending doom, you will be on your way to solving your panic.

6

Why Is Panic Happening to Me?
Some Answers

George had hard-working-man hands. He was not accustomed to being afraid, or letting fear seep into his consciousness, or talking about it. He was more familiar with trapping animals or sitting quietly in a tree, with a compound bow in his hands, hoping to see a big buck. I grew up with folks like George.

"Tell me I won't kill myself," he said. "I cannot stop thinking about it. I'm not depressed. I try to not think about suicide, but I can't get it off my mind."

I paused and wondered for a moment if this fellow's issues were above my pay grade. But with the idea that two heads are better than one, I referred him for a medication evaluation with our psychiatrist. George initially declined out of fear that an antidepressant would make him even more at risk for suicide, it did not.

George didn't look depressed; he didn't sound depressed. We did a depression test, and sure enough, it showed him free of depression. He seemed more anxious than depressed, and I said so. He agreed.

When he returned to his obsessive thoughts about suicide, I said, "Maybe that's part of the problem. We are not very good at not thinking about things. Why don't we do something different? Why don't we do a little experiment together?"

"Like what?" George asked.

"Like think about it and talk about your thoughts and fears about you killing yourself."

"How would that help?" he wanted to know.

"I'm not sure it would. Like I said, it's an experiment. What you have been doing sure hasn't been working."

George agreed.

We explored him killing himself and even visualized who would be at his funeral. He wanted no part of any of it. None of this discussion was the least bit appealing to him.

George said, "My thoughts about suicide make me feel like I'm going crazy."

"That sounds more like anxiety," I repeated. "Why don't we check that out?"

I gave him my panic test. He had only two physical symptoms: tingling in the hands and feet and a tight chest. He had three other possible symptoms: a racing heart, shortness of breath, and feeling sensations of heat. George tended to minimize (a quality I understood only too well). However, he did have eight thoughts that are common in people who have panic:

- Feelings of unreality (derealization), or detached from oneself (depersonalization)

- Fear of losing control or going crazy

- Fear of dying (that is, thoughts that you might die or have a heart attack or faint)

- Thoughts that something terribly wrong is happening

- Thoughts that these sensations are caused by some personal failing or weakness

- A feeling of fear or terror

- Dread of another attack

- Change or restriction in behavior to avoid the possibility of another attack

I asked George when this started. He related that he had been going through a lot of stress lately. He said that he had a best friend whose girlfriend broke up with him. His friend didn't seem all that upset. Then he killed himself.

"My wife recently told me she wants a divorce," he said.

"I get it. So, are you worried that you might do the same thing?"

George said, "I know I wouldn't do it, but if I lost control …"

Just because you think it, doesn't make it so. At some point, I told George a personal story:

The river was flooding as we could see from the bridge, and I had a troubling thought. What if I wanted to drive my car into the river? I told my wife of my thought and said that I want to drive down to the boat ramp and see the river and think about that thought instead of shoving it to the back of my mind.

My wife didn't object nor think I was crazy—at least she didn't say so. She knows me. She was not afraid I would suddenly have a change of character. I drove to the boat ramp near the raging river. I parked a safe distance away from and parallel to the river. I could not, even if I wanted to, drive the car on the ramp to the river. Suddenly I didn't even want to trust the brakes. It left no doubt that I for sure didn't want to drive into the swirling water.

"George," I told him, "you may have a nontraditional panic disorder. When the chemicals of panic are released, you (and many other people) think it might be a sign of losing control or going crazy, and therefore you would not be in control of your actions."

A week later, I asked him, "So how's it going?"

"I've only had thoughts of suicide three times this week," he said. "I was out scouting for deer and found a large rock by a pond. I thought that would be a good place to do something bad. It freaked me out. Instead of avoiding it, I went right up and just sat on that rock till my thoughts passed, like you've been saying."

George had been going through a lot of stress. When we go through a stressful event, our stress level goes up rapidly, but it comes down slowly, causing a buildup of stressors over time. Stress is dose related, and these doses can add up, silently stored, building toward panic. George's stress had built up on him. We discussed how his accumulated stress had led to his panic.

Most clients feel relieved to understand how accumulated stress may have led to their present problems with panic. George's panic was not a sign of him going crazy but rather a manifestation of accumulated stressors including the suicide of his friend and his own marital difficulties. With my encouragement, George switched his focus from avoiding suicidal thoughts to solving his panic.

Some stressors that add to the present stress load may even originate from events out of our conscious memory. Solving panic does not necessarily require resolving or even exploring these issues. It is enough to know many events in your past have added up and contributed to the current panic.

Discussing the history of these traumatic events may be helpful. Adults with panic disorders, when asked, frequently and readily point to feeling unsafe in one way or another during childhood.

Other relevant factors that may contribute to panic include health problems; medications; cigarettes, alcohol, or drug usage; family background; and painful or untimely losses. Heredity is, of course, a contributing factor as well.

Think about some of the stressors that you have experienced. Make a private list of the traumas and challenges that you have faced and see if the following chart makes sense to you.

Accumulated Stress Can Lead to Panic, and the Body Keeps Score

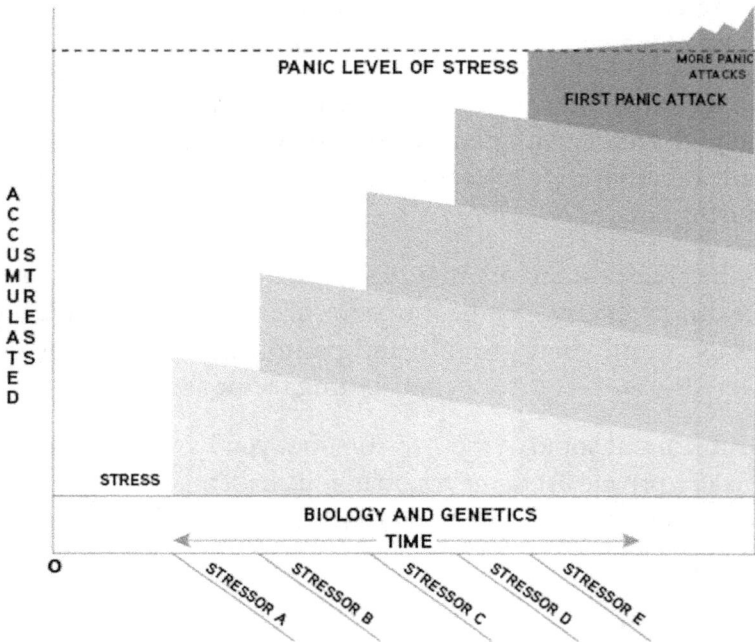

Panic Diagram

In the panic diagram, note how stress builds over time and can trigger sensations of panic. It seems that once a person's accumulated stress crosses the threshold of panic, it can recur and come out of the blue. Ways to bring down this stored level of stress are discussed later in the book.

Many events we experience add to our stress level. Some are big traumatic events, and some of them are more like a trickle charge—little things that chronically add up and build over time.

The accumulated stress model in the panic diagram can explain why people with GAD (generalized anxiety disorder), OCD (obsessive compulsive disorder), and social anxiety all struggle with panic. Each of these anxiety disorders serves to act as a "trickle charge" to keep panic fully charged and ready to happen at any moment.

- GAD is characterized by excessive, exaggerated anxiety and worry about everyday life events. These daily chronic struggles add to stress load that may end in panic.

- OCD features a pattern of unreasonable thoughts and fears (obsessions) that lead people to do repetitive behaviors (compulsions). These behaviors or rituals, like hand washing, are attempts to gain control over anxiety. Again, these daily stressors add to the accumulation of stress.

- Social anxiety disorder is intense anxiety or fear of being judged, negatively evaluated, or rejected in social situations. These fears add to the total stress load.

People with these disorders experience personally stressful events on a daily basis. The total of these stressors yields the possibility of panic attacks as a comorbid condition (in other words, occurring at the same time).

Traumatic events, like those that may lead to PTSD (posttraumatic stress disorder), quickly add to stress loads. Battlefield incidents and other sorts of traumas are also dose related. The first or second near-death experience may be managed and not lead to visible symptoms. However, as these events continue, they silently build up, and when they reach a critical mass, PTSD may develop. A person with PTSD may also experience panic due to the same accumulation.

Interpersonal conflict and drama also take their toll and add to your stress level, setting the table for the possibility of panic.

7

Understanding More about the Fight/Flight Response

Sally and her young daughter went to a movie with some other women and their daughters. She and her daughter had parked several blocks away from the theater. Once they were in line for the movie, Sally noticed a lone man with a mustache behind them. Something about him seemed troubling, but she put it out of her mind.

After the movie, one of the other mothers asked if Sally wanted a ride to her car. Sally declined and said they would just walk, although it was now dark. As soon as they started walking, Sally knew she had made a mistake in not accepting the offer of a ride. She started walking faster.

Sally glanced back; the mustached man was following. They got to the car just in time for Sally to get her daughter in the car and lock her door. Only later did she recall that on her mad dash around the car, she briefly thought about using her keys as a weapon.

As she hurriedly opened the driver's door, the man approached with both arms reaching for her. Sally fell back into the driver's seat, raising her legs for protection. Without thought, she saw her legs kicking and kicking. She didn't think about kicking her legs, they were doing what they needed to do without help from her mind. Oddly, she felt safe knowing her kicking legs were keeping the man at bay.

Later, driving away, she saw the man on the curb holding his eye as a man will do when gouged in the eye with a key. Later the police report would show he was gouged in both eyes. Sally had no memory of fighting him off with a key; she had just reacted.

We all know not to mess with a momma bear and her cub. The predator with the mustache had made a serious mistake.

This is how powerful fight-or-flight chemicals are supposed to work. Sally didn't think about or even notice her racing heart or her breathing or anything else. She just reacted. These lifesaving chemicals evolved to protect us. We still have the same wiring as our ancestors. When these powerful chemicals are released when we face a real threat, it is a blessing, not panic.

Think of a time you have been in a dangerous situation and your body's fight-or-flight response chemicals kicked in appropriately. It may be hard to remember because, when they work as intended, we hardly notice the effect they have on our bodies. When they come on voluntarily against a background that doesn't make sense, we hardly notice anything else. Here is the thing to remember: the fight-or-flight chemicals and the ways our bodies react to them are not dangerous.

Red and Me

Our dog, named Red (short for Robert Redford), is a yellow Labrador. Red is also a third-generation therapy dog. He comes to work with me frequently. Red seems to understand what is going on when he is at work and is available (or not) to each patient. He is there if wanted and remains in the background when he is not.

Red is handsome, smart, loyal, and brave. He does not just walk; he struts. He is protective of me, and vice versa.

Our Dog, Red

My wife, Mary, and I drove to one of our favorite places to walk Red. It is a beautiful, high steep bluff overlooking the Kansas River, covered with large hardwood trees and lined with serene walking trails. It is a peaceful, quiet, scenic place, perfect for appreciating nature and getting into a calm, mindful state. We had parked our car and had just let Red out. He patiently sat right next to the car door, waiting for my command to begin walking with us. Perhaps you can imagine the (unpleasant) surprise we had when an off-leash, male pit bull suddenly appeared, moving toward us.

The aggressor approached Red, walking straight up to him. The pit bull instantly stiffened, then lunged at Red, as if shot out of a cannon. The initial force of the pit bull's body blow knocked Red to the ground. The pit immediately clamped his teeth onto Red's back leg, locking down his powerful jaws.

I heard Red cry out in pain. I was mad and moved in to kick the pit bull. I aimed for and struck him in a vulnerable spot, right over his lungs. The kick got results: it knocked the wind out of him. He coughed and sputtered and let go of Red's leg, but for Red, the fight wasn't over yet. Red then attacked the pit bull back, biting it on the face and leaving lines of blood. At that point, the aggressor had enough, and it took off.

I wouldn't have thought much about the changes in my body, though, if I weren't a therapist who treats panic disorders, but as it happens, I do just that. So let's look at those first ten sensations related to panic and see which of those I experienced during the fray. I put an asterisk next to the sensations I experienced, shown in the following list:

- Palpitations, pounding heart, or accelerated heart rate*

- Sweating*

- Trembling or shaking (a noticeable internal vibration, like one might feel when standing close to a passing train whizzing by)*

- Sensations of shortness of breath*

- A feeling of choking

- Chest pain or discomfort (a feeling of tightness, but not really discomfort)*

- Nausea or abdominal distress

- Feeling dizzy, unsteady, lightheaded, or faint (This is a subtle but noticeable change, like walking out of a dark theater into the unexpectedly bright light of day. The pupils of the eyes widen automatically during the fight response, which lets in more light to improve vision.)*

- Numbness or tingling sensations (like your legs would feel after an exhilarating, high-energy snow ski run—noticeable, but not unpleasant)*

- Chills or sensations of heat (which are produced by the body's increased blood flow)*

During Red's dogfight, I experienced eight of ten sensations that are associated with panic. Notably, however, there were no misinterpretations of the experience. All of the sensations I experienced during the attack were congruent with the situation. They all made sense and were therefore not noteworthy because they fit with what was going on right then.

In fact, during the attack, I felt energized and present at the moment. My body's adrenaline was released at a time that made sense. When that happens, it makes us feel powerful or "6 foot 4 and bulletproof," as one of my 5 foot 4 patients once said so well. The natural release of those chemicals increases our physical prowess and can come in handy when we, or our loved ones, are threatened.

Using the Red and Me Story in Therapy

Sam was thirty-five. He had felt symptoms of panic and agoraphobia since grade school. This exchange took place during our first meeting.

Sam had years of therapy for his panic and the depression that it caused. I decided to give Sam my panic test anyway to be sure we were "fishing in the right pond" (and it showed that we were). He had eight of ten of the physical symptoms of panic and all but two of the associated thoughts (which were he didn't think he was dying during panic attacks, nor did he use drugs or alcohol to dull his symptoms).

When I asked Sam his understanding of the cause of his symptoms of panic, he said he had no idea, while looking as if I had just asked him a question in a foreign language. So, I told him the story about Red and me to help explain some ideas about panic to him. The story is about a particular incident, but it is similar to the kinds of memories most of us have had when facing risk.

It turned out that during Red's fight with the pit bull, I had experienced the same number of physical sensations that Sam did during his panic attacks. So I asked him, "Do you think I had panic, Sam?"

"Sure sounds like you did," he replied.

"Nope, actually, I felt pretty good and also pretty pumped up."

Sam looked puzzled and asked, "You weren't bothered by those symptoms? Why not?"

I answered, "All of those things made sense with what I was doing. I didn't have panic symptoms, just sensations, but I had the same chemicals pumping through me as you do when you have a panic attack."

Then Sam's face brightened, and he said, "But mine are bothering me because they are coming when they don't make sense!"

"They don't make sense until you understand them. That is why you are here," I said.

With that, Sam gave me a smile and a high-five, and we scheduled another appointment. Sam was now on his way to solving the panic that had plagued him for years.

Like Sally did in protecting her daughter, I had used the automatic release of my body's fight chemicals during Red's dogfight to handle a highly distressing situation. But when the fight-or-flight response is not necessary for the situation, these same automatic, lifesaving chemicals can be interpreted as panic, as Sam did.

I find that using well-timed personal stories, like the one I told Sam, can help clients quickly understand what's going on in panic. Stories can also help to clear the confusion in clients' minds and can lead to breakthroughs, those all-important "Aha!" moments.

Solving panic requires bravery on the part of clients. It also requires them to make four other essential changes, which I address in depth in the remaining chapters:

1. Changing thoughts related to knowing panic is not dangerous or a sign of weakness or insanity

2. Developing strategies for coping with and managing panic

3. Lowering the level of their accumulated stress

4. Not avoiding activities that might have caused panic in the past and reclaiming life as you are meant to live, and becoming your best self

8

Panic Disorders Are a Thinking Problem

Dave saw himself as weak. He had felt this way for so long. It was no longer a thought. The feeling was so entrenched, it had become a belief. He was in upper management with a company that required frequent travel. He dreaded travel and meetings. The presentations he had to make were preceded by weakness, shakiness, and vomiting.

He was a team player and leader, yet because of his preoccupation with panic, he did not enjoy people. He ate alone in his hotel room and dreaded the worry and nausea that would accompany him on the flight home. His weight was down to 135 pounds.

He never thought the problem was physical although he had been thoroughly checked out by many doctors. He had little voice at home; his wife raised the children. Thoughts about getting a different job and escaping never led to any action. Miserably, he soldiered on day after day.

Updating thinking is essential to solving panic. Cognitive behavioral therapy views catastrophic misinterpretation of bodily sensations to be the core problem in panic attacks. Dave believed his symptoms of panic were proof of his weakness.

These thoughts only served to bring on more chemicals. Therapy helped him break this harmful self-blaming loop.

Shifting Modes

Panic is a primitive response from the survival part of the brain. It wants to protect but is limited to fighting or avoiding. Neither option works well for solving panic. People with panic feel stuck; the more they focus on physiological sensations and catastrophize the meaning, the deeper the rut of panic.

Those who suffer from panic only want it to go away and stay away. Usually, it won't. Something else is needed. Initially, solving panic does not seem like an option. When the timing is right, asking this question, "Do you want to solve this problem or endure it?" encourages people to find the necessary resolve to engage in the work. Of course, solving panic is what they really want to do. Clients giving the answer, "I want to solve it," helps to shift them to active, problem solving. This shift is not easy, but it is doable.

At some point, solving panic requires clients to tolerate some uncomfortable feelings; they begin to take on challenges willingly rather than trying to avoid them. Therapeutic exposure techniques are effective in solving panic. Paradoxically, being willing to expose yourself (in small and graduated doses) to situations that cause fear can help you to retrain your brain to stop sending fear signals when there is no danger.

We can learn to solve panic like we do other problems: get more information, brainstorm possible options, come up with a plan, and work the plan. Then evaluate progress.

When people exaggerate the risk of panic, they feel overwhelmed. Learning about panic and how to cope with it demystifies panic and makes it solvable. Let me illustrate this observation as a formula:

$$\frac{\text{Perceived Risk}}{\substack{\text{Perceived Resources} \\ \text{(to Manage Experience)}}} = \substack{\text{Degree} \\ \text{of Anxiety}} \text{ or } \substack{\text{Panic} \\ \text{Experienced}}$$

Anxiety Formula

Remember George, the outdoorsy guy who liked to hunt and had thoughts about suicide? We continued his therapy:

I asked him, "George, on a scale of 1 to 10, how powerful did you think of panic when you first came to see me?"

"It was a 10," he said. "I couldn't stop thinking about what if I lost control of myself and I committed suicide!"

"And on the same 1 to 10 scale, how would you have rated your strength to deal with your panic? One would be you felt weak and helpless, and a 10 would be you felt strong and effective in managing your panic."

He said, "Three or 4, I guess. I can't imagine me feeling helpless. I can always ask for help. That's why I came to you!"

Where Do You Rank on the Woodward Panic Scale?

I focus on two essential factors in solving panic:

1. Knowing the associated sensations are not dangerous, although they may seem to be. Truly believing that the survival chemicals do no harm reduces fear. This idea is examined and explained in many different ways. Buying into this idea is a process. It does not happen at first blush.

2. Developing a plan to cope with and bear an attack (not a bear attack) is also fundamental.

Take a look at the Woodward Panic Scale.

THE WOODWARD PANIC SCALE

A. THE PERCEIVED STRENGTH OF PANIC

Mark the number below that rates how you experience the strength of your panic.

1 = Panic is weak/of no great concern   10 = Panic is overpowering/dreaded

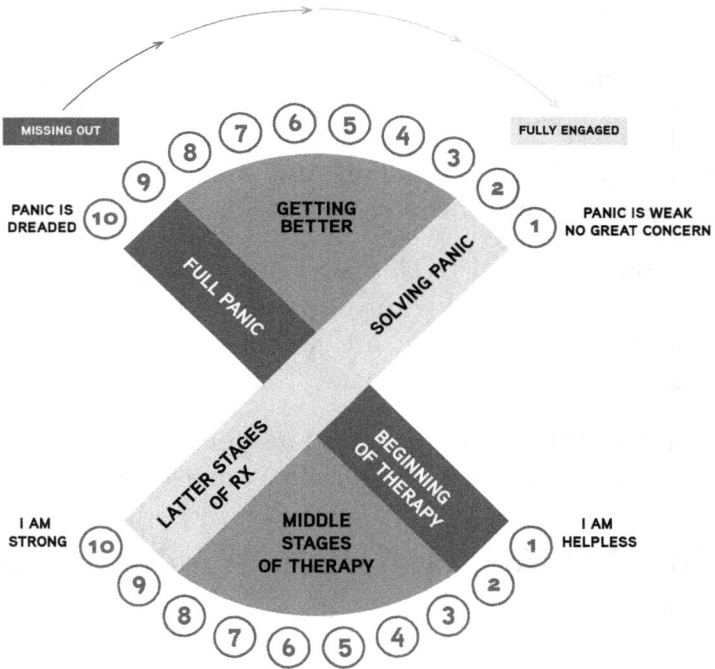

MISSING OUT   FULLY ENGAGED

PANIC IS DREADED (10)   GETTING BETTER   FULL PANIC   SOLVING PANIC   PANIC IS WEAK NO GREAT CONCERN (1)

I AM STRONG (10)   LATTER STAGES OF RX   MIDDLE STAGES OF THERAPY   BEGINNING OF THERAPY   I AM HELPLESS (1)

B. PERSONAL STRATEGY/STRENGTH FOR MANAGING PANIC

Note the number that represents how you rate your strength or ability to manage panic (without avoiding the precipitating event or using medication, drugs, or alcohol)?

1= I feel helpless/powerless   10 = I am strong/effective

Woodward Panic Scale

Solving panic boils down to reducing the perceived power panic (item A) and developing a strategy to manage panic (item B). Having a workable strategy increases confidence and the resolve to master panic.

In general, people with panic initially rate panic as strong or overwhelming, a 9 or a 10 on the strength of panic scale, which is in the full panic zone. Likewise, in the beginning, they rate themselves as helpless/powerless, a 1 or a 2 (which is also in the panic zone). Some people have done work on their own and start more in the middle of both scales.

As the therapy work begins to show results, people rate panic as less dangerous and overpowering. Their strength/strategy to cope with panic also improves. Panic presents many issues for discussion in therapy. This panic scale serves to focus the extensive work of therapy to the essentials. It helps patients understand the priorities involved in solving this issue.

After several weeks, when retested, they usually select the middle numbers, 3 through 8, on both scales. Frequent measurements on the scale track the person's progress. When people see these positive changes, they feel encouraged and know they are on the right track to solve their panic.

Reducing the fear of panic happens as panic is explained from many different angles. Once understood, the person is no longer frozen in fear and is more willing to build strategies for managing panic. Successfully managing panic further reduces the fear of it.

This synergy happens as shown on the panic scale. These two issues change and evolve together. By developing personal strategies to manage the symptoms of panic, feelings of strength and confidence grow. Progress comes rapidly.

After successful therapy, when people truly understand their panic, fear fades. They think of it as weak and rate it as a 1 or a 2, in the solving panic zone. They rate themselves as strong and effective, a 9 or a 10, also in the solving panic zone. Panic is demystified. Confidence grows. There is a dramatic shift, like finally seeing the Wizard of Oz as a plain, ordinary man when he was not hidden behind the screen.

As both of these changes occur, panic diminishes in both frequency and intensity. Then it seems to fade away.

9

Techniques to Lower Your Accumulated Stress

Early in Fran's treatment, she was motivated to get rid of panic and was spending a lot of her spare time meditating and deep breathing. She was willing to do whatever was necessary, and was working hard, too hard. Her panic was receding, but her fear of panic was unchanged. Working hard to relax is an oxymoron. Relaxing should not be hard work. She used relaxation like a ritual. She was using deep relaxation to keep panic away, like people in the movies use a crucifix to keep vampires away.

This method is not about keeping panic away.

Solving panic is learning not to be afraid of it and concentrating on how to manage it. Once your fear is gone, it will no longer dominate you.

There is considerable agreement that practicing deep relaxation is an effective technique for people with panic. For some people using only deep relaxation as a way of dealing with panic may be satisfactory. Learning to relax deeply is one component of this comprehensive approach. For most, a more comprehensive plan increases the odds of solving panic, while not just holding it at bay.

When panic is solved, there is no reason to "live small," hiding away avoiding panic. The chart diagrams the path for reducing high levels of accumulated stress.

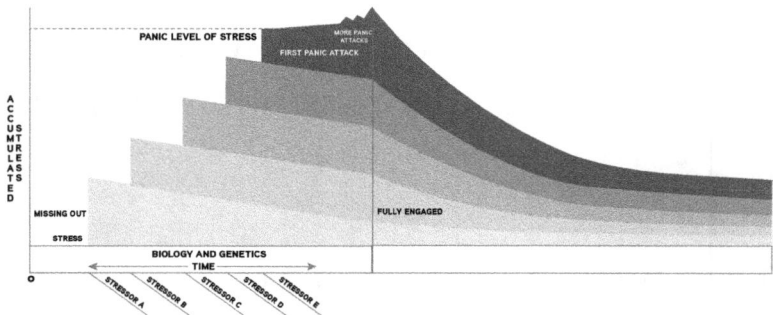

How to Lower Accumulated Stress

Wouldn't it be great if there was a way to reduce the towering level of unprocessed, stored stress that shows up as panic? Ideas on the following list can bring your accumulated stress level down:

- New strategies for thinking about and managing panic (the focus of this book)

- Antidepressant medications (may help with anxiety). The providers at our clinic find that anxious people tend to do better with minimal doses of antidepressants, and with small, infrequent increases. The problem is when people with panic are prescribed antidepressants at normal doses, like those recommended for depression, the anxious person's reaction to the medication can cause increased anxiety or panic. Our providers rarely prescribe benzodiazepines.

- Better self-care, including sleep hygiene, regular physical exercise, healthy nutrition, and more positive internal dialogue

- Psychotherapy to work on whatever else is stressful like processing emotions, problems with anger, collaborative problem solving, and improving interpersonal relationships

- Time without new stressors

- Self-calming relaxation responses (as described next)

Turning Off the Fight/Flight Response (by Learning to Turn on the Relaxation Response)

It is possible not only to turn off the fight/flight responses but also to turn on renewing healing responses that bring down the levels of stored stress. These techniques can be practiced frequently and used as a way of facing, accepting, and floating through panic attacks.

Meditation/relaxation exercises are deceptively powerful. Our bodies are willing to go into this natural, relaxed state and will do so when given an opportunity.

The biggest problem for people, in the beginning, is these exercises may feel as if you are not accomplishing much, not doing the technique very well, or simply not doing anything important. Meditation certainly may feel like it is no match for the churning in the stomach or a rapid heartbeat or labored breathing. Nevertheless, keep doing the practice without internal criticism. The ability to enter a deeply relaxed state is an ancient human skill that is practiced in different ways in all cultures. If you put in the time, relaxation comes naturally.

Another problem related to meditation and deep relaxation may develop. We try to use these methods to avoid panic rather than as an adjunct in solving it. A patient recently shared previous attempts to seek help for panic.

He said, "All we did was work on breathing techniques to help me calm down, so I would not panic." Relaxation was used to avoid experiencing panic, but not as a part of a comprehensive plan to solve the issue. Like Fran did in the opening story, it helped but did not lead to a solution.

Relaxing and Healing

Meditation/relaxation methods can be useful. They can work exceedingly well in conjunction with understanding panic and learning not to be afraid of it. The relaxation response turns off the fight-or-flight or stress response. It is associated with decreased metabolism, heart rate, blood pressure, and rate of breathing and for eliciting a feeling of calm.

In his book, *The Relaxation Response,* Herbert Benson describes Eastern practices in Western scientific terms. He understood how important relaxation is to our survival since anxiety and tension often inappropriately trigger panic in us. I believe regular elicitation of relaxation is an important skill in learning to manage and solve panic.

There is, according to Benson, no single correct approach for triggering the relaxation response. He said it is not the specific technique, per se, but the mind/body response induced that is important. He wrote that we could use any number of methods to produce the relaxation response—the key point is to do it consistently (and not get discouraged).

Whatever manner you choose to relax it should include these two qualities:

1. Break the pattern of everyday thoughts by having something on which to focus, and

2. Assume a passive attitude, noticing thoughts that interrupt concentration and letting them go without judgment. Then return to meditation.

Research shows that the relaxation response can even help our chromosomes. Let me explain. Telomeres are the "end caps" on chromosomes. The length of one's telomeres indicates physiological age, and also expected life span. Telomeres typically shorten as people age. Studies have shown that when people meditate, their telomeres get longer. Enhancing relaxed states reverses some of the effects of aging (and who doesn't want that!).

I encourage my patients and readers to practice deep relaxation daily. Then you will be ready to "float through" as a part of a strategy should you have a panic attack. These techniques can be life changing. The same methods that tamp down the fight/flight response enough to make telomeres longer can be an essential component in reducing stored stress.

Knowing how to relax is part of being a healthy human. Getting away from worry and focusing on nature can lead to increased relaxation. Ocean waves, a trickling stream, a serene lake, or watching a sunset can be a focus for mindfulness and relaxation.

Meditative states and other ways to achieve the relaxation response can help turn off the fight/flight reaction in our bodies. Relaxation responses can help us calm down and shorten our time in panic. As people learn to enter states of deep relaxation, however they choose to do it, they are developing a valuable resource for solving panic.

Five Techniques to Help Lower Accumulated Stress

1 The Relaxation Response (*1)

The idea of the relaxation response is to tap into a resource you have within yourself that turns off the fight-or-flight response and heals. The technique involves breathing slowly and focusing on a word.

To trigger the relaxation response, here are some simple steps:

- Get comfortable

- Close your eyes (it helps with focus)

- Progressively relax all your muscles. In the progression, you relax one part of the body at a time, starting with the feet. Concentrate on relaxing the feet and moving them gently. Pause for a few breaths in between each body part transition. Then move the focus of awareness in turn to other body parts: the calves, knees, thighs, buttocks, stomach, back, neck, face, and scalp.

- After focusing on progressive muscle relaxation, the next focus is on breathing. Choose a word to think in your mind with each exhale. Words like *relax, holy, peace, gratitude, forgiveness, joy,* and *love* may be used, or you may choose any word or short prayer. Focusing on the word helps to focus the mind. Breathe easily and naturally.

- Continue for ten to fifteen minutes (from the start of the relaxation to the end of breathing meditation). When random thoughts occur, notice them and say to yourself, "Oh well," internally, and let them go as you continue to focus on your breath and your word.

Permit relaxation to occur at its own pace. Do not look for perfection or be self-critical; repetition is the key. Slowly and gently open your eyes.

2 A Buddhist Breathing Meditation

One of my favorite calming exercises is a breathing meditation from a book by Thich Nhat Hanh, a Buddhist priest, *The Miracle of Mindfulness*. This simple exercise is done by slowing and controlling your breath. The following is my Americanized rendition:

The first breath starts with breathing in for one count and breathing out for one count. Next, breathe in for two counts and breathe out for two counts. The progression continues with each inhale, and each exhale becoming slower. The number of breaths is increased by one after each complete cycle.

Finally, the tenth breath is taken in for ten counts and exhaled slowly for ten counts. The exercise then closes with a return to a breath in for one count and a breath out for one count. This method is handy and easily doable. This exercise can also help to float through panic and let it pass.

3 Meditation and Mindfulness (*2)

Meditation and mindfulness are other ways of relaxing and turning off the fight/flight response. Mindfulness strategies reduce a wide range of psychological symptoms and disorders, including anxiety and panic.

Mindfulness is rational and intentional. It encourages attention to the present moment. Anxiety is mainly about worrisome things that may happen in the future. Mindfulness helps maintain an awareness of and openness to what is happening around you now. Focusing on the present moment, what we see, hear, and feel, is the basis of mindfulness. Mindfulness can be helpful in treating panic.

Some aspects of mindfulness are these:

- Focus on calming the breath and body helps to bring your attention to the present moment without judgment. It is calming to observe and describe what you see, hear, and feel in the present moment.

- Focusing your awareness helps you regulate your emotions.

Anxiety is about scary things that may happen in the future. People don't think they are crazy; they think they may be on their way to crazy. They are afraid the symptoms of panic may foretell of dire events to come. Describing and labeling feelings with words in the present moment helps to lower levels of physical arousal, which can help to diminish symptoms of panic.

Maintaining focused attention in the present moment reduces anxiety. I'm amazed by how this works. Asking simple questions like, "What are you aware of at this moment?" can help people take a breath and calm down.

Donald Altman is a psychologist and author. He used to be a Buddhist monk. One of his most well-known books is *One Minute Mindfulness*. He uses a metaphor that our minds are like a puppy. The puppy mind thinks whatever it wants to in a stream of consciousness flow. When you learn to meditate and be mindful, he describes this as training the puppy mind.

Altman's metaphor brings to mind all the love, time, patience, and discipline it takes to train a puppy to become a loyal, obedient, and loved companion. The metaphor suggests rich rewards from the investment of time practicing meditation and mindfulness. Learning how to be more mindful can be a component of floating through panic.

Staying focused on the present and having intentionally relaxed breathing dials down the fight-or-flight response. Mindfulness can help people pay attention to specific sensations and accept them, rather than fighting to control or misinterpreting them. It can also help in choosing how to think about these sensations, rather than letting the puppy mind run wild with catastrophic misinterpretations.

A senior psychiatrist at the Menninger Foundation used to say, "Mental health is having more good memories than bad memories." I encourage you to take a moment to think about one of your good memories. What was it that made the memory a good one for you?

Likely, it was meaningful because you were fully present the moment the event was happening. We could think of mental health as living a good measure of one's life mindfully.

4 Autogenic Training or Self-Hypnosis (The Schultz Technique) (*3 & *4)

Autogenic training is a relaxation technique that was first introduced by the German psychiatrist Johannes Heinrich Schultz in 1932. Schultz noticed that individuals undergoing hypnosis entered a relaxed state in which they generally experienced a predictable progression of six sensations. They are feelings of heaviness in the limbs, then warmth in the arms and legs, relaxed breathing, slowing of the pulse, warmth in the solar plexus, and coolness in the forehead.

Hypnosis requires another person to induce a trance state, while autogenic training, as the name implies, is self-administered. I find that focusing on the first three sensations (heaviness, warmth, and breathing) to be quite sufficient to induce a state of relaxation.

Here is a modified technique I propose to my patients:

To begin, choose a preferred relaxed position (sitting in a chair or a recliner or lying down on a sofa). Begin to relax your body and pay attention to your breathing.

To induce heaviness, I say this: "Go ahead and close your eyes. When you are ready, we will start. I am going to say some things to you, and then you are to think these same things quietly in your mind."

"My right arm is heavy and comfortable."

"Just notice the heaviness, and nod when you feel it so that I will know."

Then the same instructions are repeated for the left arm, right leg, and then left leg.

People with panic attacks may be hesitant to let go and give in to relaxation. If they hesitate to relax, I suggest they raise their right arm and let it fall. Usually, people will ease it down slowly. I then demonstrate the concept of heaviness by raising my arm and letting go of the muscles and letting my arm freefall to my leg "with a whack." A discussion will then ensue about gravity and the heaviness of the arm. This proof is reassuring. Who, after all, can argue with the effects of gravity?

To induce warmth, I say something like: "Now notice the warmth in your right arm and say to yourself quietly in your own mind, 'My right arm is warm and comfortable.' Just notice the warmth."

"This is the kind of warmth that comes from inside the body, as you relax, the blood flows through the circulatory system more easily. The relaxed flow of blood through the veins, arteries, and capillaries produces warmth. So, notice the warmth, your right arm is warm and comfortable."

When patients are unable to feel the warmth, I instruct them to imagine feeling the heat that comes to the hands and feet from the relaxed flow of blood through the arms and legs.

Then the same instructions are given with the left arm, the right leg, and then the left leg.

The beauty of the Schultz technique is that these changes are naturally going to happen in people when they relax. You only need to notice the sensations. The arm is heavy; you only have to feel the heaviness. The same is true of the warmth that comes with relaxation, and the same is true of the relaxed breathing. Attention is focused, at the moment, on each particular sensation that is suggested.

To induce relaxed breathing, the third stage, I say, "Now, notice your relaxed breathing and say, quietly, in your mind, 'My breathing is slow and steady.' Just notice your slow, relaxed breathing."

Again, the intention is to focus attention now on the breath. The Schultz technique is quite different from other methods of relaxation or meditation in that the relaxed breathing and the relaxation response are both byproducts of the guided focus on feeling the heaviness and warmth.

When using autogenic relaxation training, relaxation tends to happen quite naturally and profoundly. Even people who have a difficult time developing relaxed breathing do it naturally, without effort, during the first two stages, heaviness and warmth. By the third breathing stage, usually the person will already have relaxed breathing.

Notice how the focus on the moment increases mindfulness. Autogenic training helps you shift your focus, in the moment, on the physical sensations of heaviness, warmth, and breathing.

I have been doing hypnosis for years. Many of the aspects of autogenic training, like the Schultz technique, fit nicely with what happens during actual hypnotic sessions. I teach people to do autogenic training. Then they do it on their own. The Schultz method is an excellent way to achieve the relaxation response.

Visualization

By using autogenic training, you may be able to visualize yourself making positive changes in managing your panic. I might say something like this, "See if you can get an image in your mind, from your own eyes, not like watching it on a screen, how you would look and feel making these positive changes that you seek to make." Envision positive changes as you say these affirmations:

- I am improving.

- I am relaxed.

- I am accomplishing my goals.

- I am gaining confidence each day.

- I am changing my understanding of panic.

- I can imagine myself solving my panic.

5 The Kyrie (also called The Christ Chant) (*5)

The Kyrie is a formal prayer used in Christianity. (If you are spiritually inclined, you may select a prayer of any religion, rather than this specific Christian prayer.)

Here is the prayer and the technique:

Christ have mercy (say this quietly to yourself when you inhale).

Lord have mercy on me (say this to yourself when you exhale).

Say this over and over to yourself, coordinating it with your breathing. Think about the meaning of the words as you say them. It is possible to have a visualization when doing this prayer; be open to this possibility. Do this for approximately ten to twelve minutes.

I recommend you practice a relaxation technique daily, in one form or another. This can take as little as two to fifteen minutes per day. It is a good thing to do as a bedtime routine, and it helps to get a good night's sleep. Enhancing your ability to sleep well also helps to reduce anxiety and panic.

Notes for Chapter 9

(*1) **Relaxation response**: While it might seem that your body and brain aren't doing much when you're on break, relaxing triggers a flurry of genetic activity that is responsible for some important health benefits. When you really relax—using any type of meditative technique such as deep breathing, yoga or prayer—the genes in your body switch to a different mode. Genes that counteract the chemical effects of stress kick in, while those responsible for driving more anxious and alert states take a backseat. And a new study shows that long-term practice of relaxation techniques can significantly enhance these genetic benefits. Dr. Herbert Benson, Director Emeritus of the Benson-Henry Institute and an associate professor of medicine at Harvard Medical School, first defined the relaxation response in the early 1970s and led the latest genetic investigation published in the journal *PLOS One*.

(*2) **Meditation**: Meditation seems to affect longevity of the physical body in a few different ways, starting at the cellular level. Scientists have isolated length of telomeres and telomerase as indicators of cellular aging. Our cells contain chromosomes, or sequences of DNA. Telomeres are "protective protein caps" at the end of our DNA strands that allow for continued cell replication. The longer the telomere, the more times a cell can divide and refresh. Each time a cell replicates, its telomere length, and therefore its lifespan, gets shorter in a natural aging process. "Meditation's positive impact appears to be even more far-reaching, potentially adding years to our lives and improving cognitive function well into old age." (From Rina Deshpande, *The Science of Meditation's Effects on Aging* (2016) in www.huffpost.com.)

(*3) To review the **Schultz Technique,** read the original material presented by Wolfgang Luthe and Johannes Heinrich Schultz in the book *Autogenic Therapy*.

(*4) Biofeedback practitioners integrate basic elements of **autogenic imagery** and have simplified versions of parallel techniques that are used in combination with biofeedback. This was done at the Menninger Foundation by Elmer Green, Steve Fahrio, Patricia Norris, Joe Sargent, Dale Walters, and others. They incorporated the hand-warming imagery of autogenic training and used it as an aid to develop thermal biofeedback.

(*5) Part Four of the Catechism of the Catholic Church, which is dedicated to Christian prayer, devotes paragraphs 2665-2669 to the subject of prayer to Jesus.

"The invocation of the Holy Name of Jesus is the simplest way of praying always. When the Holy Name is repeated often by a humbly attentive heart, the prayer is not lost by heaping up empty phrases but holds fast to the Word and 'brings forth fruit with patience.' This prayer is possible 'at all times' because it is not one occupation among others, but the only occupation: that of loving God, which animates and transfigures every action in Christ Jesus."

10

Avoiding Panic Does Not Solve It (Panic Should Be Solved, Not Just Made Better)

Betty had stayed home for a long time, so long that she could no longer remember the reason. She never went to a store or restaurant and hadn't been to a doctor in thirty years (despite plenty of urging). No signs of panic were present as long as she stayed home; she didn't experience much discomfort.

Betty's face had lost its plasticity and expression. Her life was quiet. In the beginning, her pale face appeared to be almost lifeless. She wasn't very interested in making changes. She had grown comfortably uncomfortable.

Tom, her husband, set the appointment and always came with her to my office. He longed for her to be a full companion and life partner again. They had children and grandchildren in Colorado, and he wanted to be involved with them.

I told Betty and Tom a story about a fellow I had treated in a stop-smoking group years before. I volunteered to help with the group at the local health department. One of the men in the group, I'll call him Mr. Dollar, was sixty-eight years old and had been smoking heavily for sixty years! He was a pleasant, happy fellow whose body had been decimated by smoking. Yet he could think of no reason to stop.

I asked him if he could think of anyone who would be happy if he quit smoking. He smiled and said, "Yes, it would make my wife very happy." We agreed he would stop smoking, not for himself but her.

He was able to quit smoking and I know he did quit smoking because he called every month for several years to tell me so. I said, "So, Betty, who could you make happy by making these changes?" We all three knew the answer. Betty just smiled.

We discussed how expert she had become at avoiding being uncomfortable and how that skill had made her a prisoner in her own house. I explained how she needed to tolerate some discomfort and spend time away from home to solve this problem.

With reluctance, she agreed to homework assignments that at first made her uncomfortable. She decided to do things that had become unnatural for her.

We started by assigning her to take rides with her husband in his truck. Tom bought a new truck largely for these outings. He was both motivated and patient for the changes that he knew she was making for him. Each week the rides grew longer. We would discuss what she saw and was aware of during the outings. They would tell about seeing red-tailed hawks, flocks of geese, and cows that were nursing baby calves. She would anticipate with pleasure seeing buffalo when the herd was grazing near the highway as they often were. She described the farm and ranch smells as they took time to pause and inhale them.

I have to admit that sometimes I wondered why I was getting paid for the slow pace of this work. It was, I suppose, a version of mindfulness. People change at their pace, not at my pace, and I'm okay with that.

Eventually, she agreed to go to a restaurant and not to leave until her uncomfortableness passed. To her great surprise, she enjoyed it. After that, she seemed to welcome the homework, and her life became more colorful and interesting. After a year of therapy, she and her husband took a successful trip to Colorado. Shortly after, they moved there.

Reinforcement Strategies

It is not a good strategy to reinforce negative behavior. There is a colorful story from the 1970s about former President Richard Nixon "training" his dog named Checkers. Legend has it that President Nixon was meeting with then–Secretary of State Henry Kissinger in the Oval Office when Checkers began chewing the carpet. The president first swore angrily at the dog, then commanded the dog to stop chewing the carpet, and finally resumed his discussion with Kissinger.

The dog, however, promptly began attacking the rug once more. There was another round of swearing, and, after a pause, Checkers again used the Persian as a chew toy. Seeing this, Nixon stopped talking to Kissinger, took a dog biscuit from his desk drawer, and gave it to Checkers, while also commenting, "Checkers needs something to chew on, I guess."

At which point, Kissinger immediately retorted, "Congratulations, Mr. President, you have just taught your dog to chew on the rug."

It is essential to be selective about which behaviors to reinforce when solving panic. Attempts to avoid the problem, such as leaving the scene, or reflexively taking a pill, are like Nixon teaching the dog to chew the carpet. This reinforces the wrong behavior; it increases insecurity and self-doubt.

A patient once said to me, "When I get these symptoms, I want them to go away. So I leave wherever I am." This is common, but not a way to master panic.

The truth is that without the accompanying catastrophic misinterpretations, the symptoms of panic will naturally dissipate after a time, all on their own. The challenge is to change scary thoughts that accompany the episode, rather than finding ways to avoid them.

It is essential to learn not to avoid whatever triggered the panic. When panic happens in a store, there is an urge to race away. People with panic are encouraged not to leave the store until their symptoms fade. If a person leaves the situation and the panic symptoms go away, the wrong (avoiding) behavior is reinforced, just like Nixon did with Checkers.

There is an understandable yet fundamental flaw in many well-intended approaches to panic. People who are experiencing panic want it to stop. It is that simple. Naturally, they also want to feel comfortable and safe. Unfortunately, however, until people understand panic, they dread the thoughts and feelings associated with it. They easily slide into maladaptive safety-seeking strategies to avoid their panic.

Betty was an expert at avoiding panic. She had engineered life to keep panic away. Paradoxically, in order to solve panic, people need to do activities that are temporarily uncomfortable. For Betty this meant getting out of the house and learning to tolerate some discomfort.

Avoiding Panic

Avoiding anxiety-provoking situations to be sure has a certain commonsense logic to it. However, the results of trying to stay safe paradoxically deliver isolation and misery. Focusing on trying to prevent any discomfort results in the opposite effect.

People try many ways to avoid panic or make it go away. They often request (and are offered) powerful and often addicting medications, such as benzodiazepines. Stops at the liquor store and trips to the emergency room are efforts to seek relief from the frightening symptoms of panic. Unfortunately, however, none of these strategies do anything constructive to solve the central problem. Avoiding situations or sensations that you fear will cause you more panic in the long run.

When you avoid, or retreat from a feared situation, it does provide some relief, but it also makes you feel more anxious about the future and more likely to avoid it again. This is not what we want to do.

One woman with panic would race outside to smoke when she felt fear coming on. Psychologically, she gave credit to the cigarette for making the alarm go away. She felt grateful for the cigarette and continued to think of herself as powerless. To change this, she agreed to homework—facing the panic symptoms and thinking, "I'll accept this and let it happen, and it will pass," while relaxing and breathing until it passed. She also agreed not to smoke until ten minutes after she was again calm.

Many people take flight, reducing the intensity of the symptoms of panic by carefully crafting restricted lives. They avoid anything they fear will make them uncomfortable or trigger an attack. They may avoid travel, social gatherings, shopping, or parties where any or all of which might increase the possibility of having panic.

Some people isolate or become irritable. Others become dependent. Many people with unsolved panic end up with depression that can lead to self-neglect, medical complications, and even premature death. It's not the panic that causes this; it is efforts to avoid panic.

Some may keep doing things, but do so on guard, and under duress, continually worried about panic striking again. One clue that panic is not solved is a prescription bottle of Xanax or other drugs close at hand.

Using quick-acting chemicals to cope with anxiety or panic eventually reduces a person's natural problem-solving abilities.

Using marijuana separates you from your feelings as it dissociates your thinking from the meaningful world. Many people smoke to deal with their anxieties and to get in a better mood. This is self-medicating, but it also turns off our reasoning processes.

Using substances to calm down and "dumb you down" are the very opposite of using cognitive abilities to solve panic. The short-term gain of numbing eventually causes long-term pain and offers no real solution.

You have not solved panic as long as you remain fearful of another attack. If avoiding panic worked, most people would have been cured a long time ago.

The Paradox of Facing the Problem of Panic to Solve It

Solving panic is like learning to play golf. While giving a lesson, a golf pro said, "If it feels natural, it's not golf!" It seems logical that if you want to hit a golf ball a long way, you should swing hard. Those who play golf well also know the smooth, effortless swing produces the best results. Swinging like you are killing snakes results in lost balls and high scores, I keep reminding myself.

Like golf, solving panic does not feel natural. It is not natural to accept something that feels as overwhelming and as frightening as panic and allow it to pass through and then flow out of your body. The treatment of panic is not natural; it is in fact counterintuitive.

Interoceptive exposure is purposely bringing on a troubling sensation that is related to a symptom of panic. People who are afraid of having a racing heart may be asked to jog in place to expose them to the very sensation that they fear. This is to desensitize them to their fear of a rapid heartbeat. A person must have a medical clearance to know there is no underlying heart problem in order to use this method.

Thankfully, understanding the nature and biology of panic helps to make logical sense of this approach that initially feels so unnatural. You can learn to use the rational, problem-solving part of your brain to take charge during panic. Knowing what is going on in the body during an attack and not getting thrown off track helps to calm the body.

Paradoxically accepting panic instead of avoiding it at first seems like a leap of faith. It takes courage. Understanding the nature and purpose of the fight/flight chemicals and knowing that they do you no harm helps you make that leap, like Betty did. Once you've practiced accepting the sensations of panic instead of avoiding them, you'll come to understand that the problem is not the sensations, but your effort to avoid them that has kept you agitated.

11

Catastrophic Thoughts Cause Panic (Don't Believe Everything You Think)

When Jenni was upset, she thought of herself as stupid. She worked as hard as anyone but seldom seemed to do better than a B in school. She thought it might have to do with all of the radiation used in treating a brain tumor at age eight, but it probably had more to do with test anxiety, the focus of our work together.

The first time she took the computerized certification exam to be a registered dietitian, she panicked and missed the cutoff for passing by one point. The second time she took the exam, her anxiety was worse and, consequently, so was her score. She said her mind just went blank and confessed that this wasn't a new problem for her, but it was getting worse.

I asked her, "What were your thoughts when you didn't pass?"

"Why am I just so dumb, so stupid and dumb? I'm going to die if I don't pass that test!"

"Jenni," I asked, "would you do a little experiment with me?"

She said she would.

"Jenni, imagine you are talking to a little eight-year-old girl in that chair over there," I said as I pointed to an empty chair, "and say the same things to that imaginary girl that you just said to yourself."

"You are going to die if you don't pass that test."

"My God! I'd never say that to anyone!" She got the point.

"No pressure there," I said. "I'm sure that threat and self-criticism don't help your test-taking abilities. That's a lot for anyone to bear."

The next test, she was less critical of herself and used self-calming techniques and mindfulness. She passed her test.

How you think about panic is the ball game. When panic sensations activate without apparent danger, people misinterpret them as something terrible. Once misinterpreted by the mind, the body responds to these horrific interpretations of threat with an increasing cascade of chemicals and symptoms.

The symptoms of panic, as I have noted earlier, include palpitations, sweating, trembling, shortness of breath, a feeling of choking, chest pain, feeling dizzy or lightheaded, numbness, or tingling sensations (paresthesia), chills, or heat sensations. These powerful sensations invite catastrophic misinterpretations, which are misguided attempts to make sense out of the sensations.

When these changes in the body happen out of context, with no apparent danger and for no apparent reason, people easily misinterpret the sensations as terrible. Those kinds of thoughts, though, only make matters worse. The thoughts seem to come in three different varieties: psychiatric, self-critical, or medical, or some combination of the three.

Let's review the types of thoughts that can cause panic:

Psychiatric

- "I'm losing control or going crazy."
- "I'm not coming back from this."
- "I'm losing my grip on reality."
- "I feel detached from myself."

Self-critical

- "I should control my symptoms and not let them happen or show."
- "I don't want anyone to know."
- "I'm not good enough."
- "I'm a failure" (or other self-critical thoughts).
- "I'm not as strong as other people."
- "If I don't control this, I must be weak."
- "If I panic, it is a sign of my inadequacy."

Medical

- "Something undiagnosed is wrong with me."
- "I'm going to die."
- "Something terrible is happening to me."
- "I must be having a heart attack."
- "I need to go to another specialist to be reevaluated."
- "Where is the nearest Mayo Clinic?"

Jenni had the self-critical type.

To Solve Panic, Learn to Replace Catastrophic Thoughts

The time to practice thinking about panic is when you are feeling calm. You need to practice and rehearse different ways of thinking about panic. Baseball players don't practice batting when they are in a game. They practice well before the game; likewise, we need to practice how to think differently about panic before it is game on, and it begins.

I encourage you to study these reassuring facts and strategies that you can use to replace your catastrophic thoughts. Feel free to reword them and make them personal or add any other ideas that would work best to help you stay grounded. Then write the ideas that make the most sense to you on index cards or enter them into your smartphone and keep them handy. Practice thinking about these ideas and rehearse them by saying them to yourself. These ideas will help you hang on to rationality when the surge of blood and chemicals races through your body.

- I'm not in danger.
- I'm having a false alarm.
- I'm not losing control.
- My body is responding to danger that is not really there.
- I'm not going crazy.
- I am sane, and I know what is happening.
- These confusing symptoms "invite" me to misinterpret them.
- I am not alone in this (even though I feel alone).
- This is treatable.
- I'm not going to die.
- I am not hopeless; I have hope.

- Nothing terrible is happening.

- It is just my body's survival chemicals coming at the wrong time.

- I'm not having this because I am weak or because of a personal failing. I'm having a false alarm.

- My self-criticism and self-doubt increase panic.

- I am strong, and I can solve this panic problem.

- Panic has been getting in my way because I haven't understood it.

- Panic is a bluff. My physical feelings are not medically significant.

- Panic is just chemistry and thoughts.

- I cannot control chemistry directly, but I can manage my thoughts, which, in turn, control chemistry.

- Panic attacks reach a peak within five to twenty minutes and then dissipate (if I believe scary thoughts, I will prolong this panic attack).

- I know once the fight-or-flight chemicals are released, the sensations or symptoms cannot be willed out of my body.

- Emotional reasoning is confusing feelings as facts.

- Feelings are not facts.

- The symptoms of panic may feel dangerous, but they are not dangerous.

- I know panic starts with chemicals released in my body, and I know, with time, the sensations they bring will pass.

About the Chemicals of Panic (the Right Thing at the Wrong Time)

These fact-based thoughts work to calm the body. The way you think *does* determine what happens next. These ideas each describe panic from a slightly different perspective.

- This state of alert, to fight or flee, is an evolutionary survival response, and it is there to protect me.

- With this alert, adrenaline flows into my bloodstream. Adrenaline is a combination of chemicals (epinephrine, norepinephrine, dopamine, and cortisol) released by the adrenal gland.

- These chemicals are there to make me more powerful.

- This adrenaline is a friend and could protect me in a dangerous situation.

- If there were a real danger, I would be glad for all of the chemicals churning through my body because they would make me stronger and faster.

- If there were a real physical threat, I would likely not think of these sensations as unusual or dangerous because the changes in my body would make sense in that situation.

- My body would be doing the right thing if there were a real danger.

- During a panic, my body responds as it would during a physical threat, but these reactions are incongruent with the situation at hand.

- My body is doing the right thing at the wrong time.

- The physiological surge of chemicals during a panic is my body's normal response to danger.

12

Strategies to Get Through Panic Attacks

Fran had been fighting to control her panic for a long time. Accepting it seemed foreign and unnatural. In spite of her best efforts, she would struggle against it. In a therapy session, I said, "Fran, I am going to tell you a story, and I want you to imagine yourself in this story."

"Okay."

"Fran, you have a broken ankle, and you go to an orthopedic surgeon. He tells you the good news first. He can fix you up. Then the bad: the fix will require surgery. He says he wants to make sure your heart is healthy enough for the procedure, so he sends you down to the lab. You are on crutches, and you take the elevator down.

"You walk in and see three treadmills, and you think to yourself this is never going to work because I cannot walk on the equipment with crutches. You say as much to the lab technician. She informs you it is not a problem because they will give you a shot to make your heart rate increase, and then they can test your heart."

Then I asked Fran, "Guess what is in the shot they are going to give you?"

"Adrenaline?" she guessed.

"Pretty much like that," I affirmed. "What would you do?"

"I might be a little scared, but it would just go away, so I would give in to it and relax," she said.

At this point, Fran started to cry. I asked what she was feeling, and she said, "Bingo. I get it."

Then she said, "I feel relieved. I need to do the same thing if I have panic and I haven't been. I've been fighting to keep it away. I need to accept panic and give in to it by relaxing as you have been encouraging me to do."

One patient's thought that worked best for her was this: "This will soon pass, it always does."

Another patient replaced frantic thoughts, such as, "Oh my God, here it comes" and "Where is my medicine?" with the idea, "God, help me through this." She repeated this to herself, and sure enough, it became true.

Another fellow named Joe worked long hours in a manufacturing job; he averaged putting in about 72 hours per week, which had, no doubt, contributed to his current struggle with panic.

With the help of therapy, Joe was able to make a shift in his thinking about panic. He changed from thinking, "I'm going to die" and "I can't breathe," to thinking instead, "This is natural, it is just my fight-or-flight chemicals coming at the wrong time." As his thoughts and beliefs changed, the terror of panic lost its grip on him.

Thoughts and Strategies

Here are some additional thoughts and strategies to think about that may bring comfort during a panic attack:

- I'm not going to fight this. I'll accept it, and it will pass.

- Fighting (symptoms) only releases more fight-or-flight chemicals.

- Paradoxically, the more I fight the panic, the deeper I sink into it, as though in quicksand.

- Fighting it doesn't help solve panic.

- I'm going to notice my sensations and learn enough about them not to be afraid.

- I am accepting the idea that these sensations are part of a self-protective mechanism that is simply coming at the wrong time.

- These sensations will soon pass if I keep my head on straight.

- Even if I feel like I need to hold myself together, I don't need to. It is just a feeling.

- I am already together (even though I may not feel like it at the moment).

- I couldn't fall apart even if I tried.

- I'm just going to give in and relax (as best I can) and let these chemicals work their way out of my body (and these thoughts work their way out of my mind).

- I am going to accept these sensations.

- I need to float through this by breathing and relaxing and letting time pass.

- Breathing slowly induces feelings of calm and relaxation.

- If I feel like I cannot breathe, then I need to exhale all of my air, then breathe in.

- I'm going to concentrate on exhaling to make room for air to come in.

- I'll practice these relaxing breaths when I'm calm and be ready to do the same to float through if I panic.

- When I use my skills to go into a state of relaxation, I help my body turn off the fight/flight response.

- Relaxation and time help flush the chemicals out of my body.

- I'm not going to run from my anxiety.

- For now, I'll think clearly, get through this and let it pass and not diagnose myself or call myself critical names.

- I'll talk to people and reach out for information, resources, and support.

- The more I'm learning about panic, the less risk I feel it holds for me.

- As I develop more confidence in my resources and strategies, I feel stronger. Soon panic will no longer have a hold on me.

13

Expect to Solve Panic and Become Your Best Self

Jack was twenty and dreaded the life ahead of him. Currently, his life consisted of working with computers by day and crying at night in his bedroom at his parents' home. His tears were about his disabling panic and his thoughts on his weakness.

Both Jack and his father were outdoorsmen. Jack seemed to admire his father more than anyone. He thought his father was a perfectionist, a highly competent one, although his father could also be irritable and critical. I don't imagine crying went over well in the house, except for in the privacy of his bedroom.

Initially, Jack frequently canceled his therapy appointments. I wanted to work with him, but I told him I wouldn't keep seeing him if he didn't keep his appointments after he made them. Ironically, that seemed to give Jack the motivation to commit to the process.

Jack learned about his panic and also how to cope with it. He learned how to think about it, and himself, more realistically. He stopped crying. Jack started jogging, joined a local running club, got more serious about playing his guitar, and started taking lessons again. For the first time, he thought about moving out and wondered aloud what his parents would think when he did.

Before therapy, when Jack went out of town on a business trip, he did what was required and then retreated to his hotel room. The last time he was on a business trip, however, he and three women took a walk together along the river and he serenaded the ladies with his guitar. He told the story as if it were no big deal, as just another day in his life now.

Compared to how he was before solving the problem of his panic, it was a big deal. Both Jack and I recognized how much more confidence he had now. The process had taken two months; what a difference just two months had made in Jack's life.

When clients solve their panic, they get way better. When you solve your panic, you can get way better too.

Untreated panic truly baffles people. Ironically, during an episode of panic, people experience the same chemicals that evolved to protect them as a threat to their life or their sanity. How disorienting it is when it feels like one's very survival is at risk. It convinces people that they have a serious medical problem or a psychiatric problem, or that they are just terribly weak and incompetent. However, those thoughts reflect not only a lack of understanding of what panic is, but also serve to make the symptoms of panic worse.

People who solve their panic are no longer afraid of the symptoms and sensations they experience. Mainly, they have learned to understand and believe in two important things. First, they now know, in their minds and their bodies, that panic is not dangerous. Second, they have developed, practiced, and internalized effective strategies to get through a panic attack. Both of these critical changes help alleviate their previous self-doubt and self-criticism that are so prevalent in people with panic.

It is the elegant simplicity of this therapeutic approach that makes it work. Changing your understanding of panic can also work for you, just like it has worked for Jack and many others.

When you are caught in the grip of panic, your safety and survival concerns are dominant and take over completely. Your crisis, during a panic attack, is fundamentally about staying alive and staying sane.

In the field of mental health, a well-known model of human growth is neatly conceptualized in Maslow's Hierarchy of Needs. A modified version of Maslow's theory is used in the following figure to explain how panic can be so debilitating, on the one hand, and yet, on the other hand, can also be solved so rapidly.

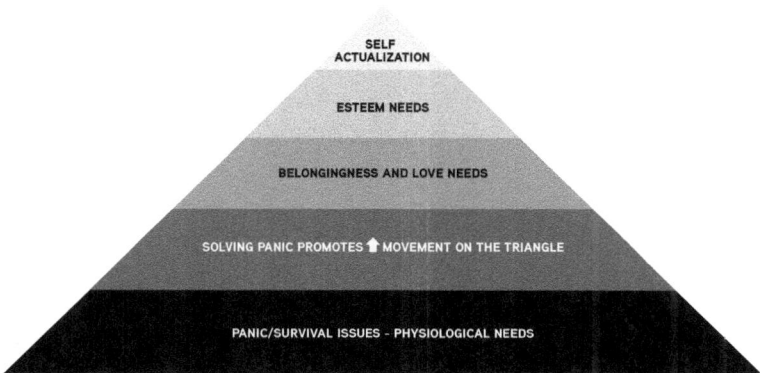

BASED ON MASLOW'S HIERARCHY OF NEEDS

Panic Diagram Based on Maslow's Hierarchy of Needs

Survival needs are on the base level of the triangle, including breathing and staying alive and sane. Panic threatens these primary needs.

Maslow's theory suggests that each stage of need must be met, more or less, before progression to the next higher level can occur. This same concept can help us understand people who have panic. When panic strikes, their attention is focused on surviving. Their struggle to survive takes precedence over everything else. This fundamental concern keeps people with panic "stuck" at the base level of the triangle.

This therapeutic approach, however, helps people get unstuck from the terror their panic brings and helps them to be able to progress rapidly to new ways of understanding coping with this problem. They learn to believe they aren't going to die or go crazy from their panic, and they learn strategies they can use to deal effectively with their panic attacks.

Solving panic offers real relief from your immediate survival concerns. Although the concept is confusing at first, you can overcome your fears quickly once you truly understand the protective, evolutionary purpose of our body's fight/flight chemicals. The same chemicals, designed to save our lives, are simply being triggered at the wrong time in a panic attack. As you learn to understand that and to develop strategies for enduring a panic attack, you can quickly begin to unravel the mystery of panic.

When people with panic learn to implement this method, they develop confidence that they're going to be able to breathe and stay safe and sane. Finally, feeling safe propels them to move quickly to higher levels of functioning. The frequent and remarkable recovery you and others can experience curiously seems to happen almost without people noticing it. Panic just fades away, and new interests come along to take its place.

Bring a New Sheriff to Town

Our evolutionary fight-or-flight chemicals have helped us to survive, but when these same chemicals are misinterpreted as being dangerous, panic results. So these chemicals are not the problem. The problem is how we think about those chemicals when they come at the wrong time. Panic, then, is primarily a thinking problem.

Our problem-solving abilities have also evolved. It is this problem-solving part of the brain (the new sheriff) that we need to use to solve panic.

Claire Weekes, the physician/author mentioned earlier who was the first to solve her panic and write clearly about it, described panic as "a few medically insignificant chemicals that are temporarily out of place in the brain." She learned how to accept, rather than to fight, the resulting sensations of panic caused by the chemicals. She knew the chemicals did her no harm (even though initially they do feel alarming).

Learning to achieve thoughts like these are the goals of treatment. They indicate no longer being afraid of panic and having no need to restrict life to avoid it. You are then free to become your best self. As your panic is solved, you can explore new interests and reclaim your life.

A principle of science states that energy can neither be created nor destroyed; energy can only be transferred or changed from one form to another. A person with panic has abundant, although unproductive, energy. In that form, they only experience it as misery.

Effective treatment transforms the misery of panic into a new form. As panic is solved, that altered energy makes life less frightening and living fully more possible.

Solving panic is a transformation.

About the Author

Jim Lance Woodward began working at the renowned Menninger Foundation when he was eighteen years old. He earned a master's degree in social work from the University of Denver and worked as a therapist at the Boulder County Mental Health Center for several years.

After returning to Kansas he took advantage of many learning opportunities at the Menninger Foundation including studying cognitive behavioral therapy for six years. He also studied CBT at the Beck Institute. He holds advanced certification in Eye Movement Desensitization and Reprocessing (EMDR) and is also skilled in Gestalt and Family Systems Therapy. He continues to work as president of Shunga Creek Mental Health Services.

Jim enjoys cycling and has a lifelong interest in strength and fitness training.